ESCAPE FROM CHILDHOOD

BOOKS BY JOHN HOLT

How Children Learn
How Children Fail
The Underachieving School
What Do I Do Monday?
Freedom and Beyond
Escape from Childhood

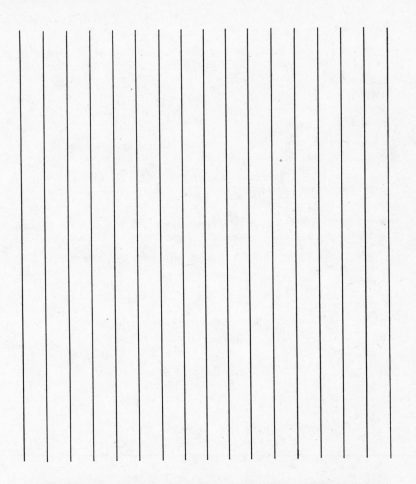

ESCAPE FROM CHILDHOOD

John Holt

E. P. DUTTON & CO., INC. NEW YORK | 1974

Acknowledgment is made for permission to quote from the folowing:

"Another Unhappy Year at Willowbrook," by Robin Reisig. Reprinted by permission of *The Village Voice*. Copyright by The Village Voice, Inc., 1972.

"Childhood Abuse Held a Leading Killer" by Jane Brody; November 3, 1972 Article by Enid Nemy; and "Drug Raid Victims . . ." by Andrew Malcolm. Copyright © 1973/1972 by The New York Times Company. Reprinted by permission.

Children in Trouble by James Howard. Reprinted by permission of David McKay Company, Inc.

"Children's Rights: The Latest Crusade" and "Less School—More Work." Reprinted by permission from *TIME*, The Weekly Newsmagazine. Copyright Time Inc.

Man's World, Woman's Place by Elizabeth Janeway. Reprinted by permission of William Morrow and Company. Copyright © 1971 by Elizabeth Janeway.

Medicine and Society by Henry Miller. Reprinted by permission of The Clarendon Press. Oxford, England. Copyright © 1973 by Oxford University Press.

Library of Congress Cataloging in Publication Data

*Holt, John Caldwell, 1923_*
Escape from childhood.

1. Child study. 2. Children—Management.
3. Youth. I. Title.
HQ769.H725   301.43'15   73_18060

Published simultaneously in Canada by Clarke, Irwin & Company
Limited, Toronto and Vancouver
ISBN: 0-525-099557
Designed by The Etheredges

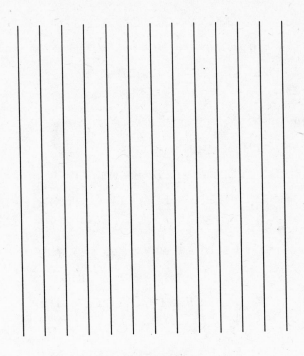

CONTENTS

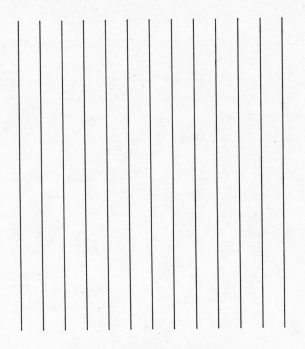

ACKNOWLEDGMENTS

In thinking over many years about children, their relations with adults, and their place in society, I have been much helped by my sisters, Jane Pitcher and Susan Bontecou, and my friends and colleagues Peggy Hughes, Terry Kros, and Margot Priest. Margot has also discussed this book with me at length in every stage of its preparation and has added valuable ideas and insights to it.

It was Paul Goodman, through his book *Growing Up Absurd,* and later Peter Marin, through his article "The Open Truth and Fiery Vehemence of Youth," who first gave me the thought that modern childhood might not be a good idea. It was J. H. van den Berg, through his book *The Changing Nature of Man,* who first suggested that it was quite a new idea. Since then I have learned much from what is becoming a standard text on the history of modern childhood, Philip Aries' *Centuries of Childhood.* I have also found additional useful information and insights in Elizabeth Janeway's *Man's World, Woman's Place,* Shulamith Firestone's *The Dialectics of Sex,* and many books and articles about the young by Edgar Friedenberg.

To all of these, and to the many others who have discussed these ideas with me, I give my sincerest thanks.

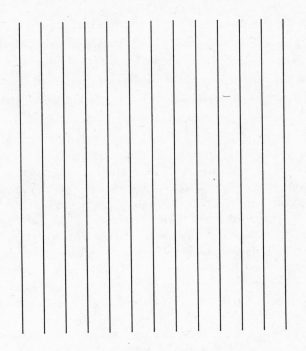

PREFACE

Early in his book *The Changing Nature of Man,* the Dutch historical psychologist J. H. van den Berg, tells a story about the philosopher Martin Buber. After a lecture, Buber was continuing the discussion with a few friends in a restaurant. A middle-aged Jew came in, introduced himself, sat down, and listened to the discussion with great interest, though without speaking. At the end of the discussion he came to Buber to ask him some questions about a young man that his daughter was thinking of marrying. The question most on his mind was: should his future son-in-law become a barrister or a solicitor. Buber replied that, as he did not know the young man in question, he could not tell—and indeed, would not be able to tell even if he did know him. The man thanked Buber and left, clearly disappointed.

Of this incident van den Berg writes:

> In this conversation an ancient certainty—the certainty that wise men are men who know—was shattered by a modern inability. Buber ought to have said, "He should become a solicitor" or "He should become a barrister."
>
> "How could he know?" cried out Buber's modern contemporary—as if action were founded on knowledge. Of course Buber could not know. But nobody asked him to know. What he had been asked for was advice—judgement, not knowledge. Is not the truth, truth in the relation between man and man, basically the effect of a fearlessness toward the other person? Is not the truth, above all, a result, a made up thing, a creation of the sage? The person who knows creates the future by speaking.

In our times people seem to define truth more and more as the result of some sort of "scientific" experiment, with things weighted and measured and arranged in neat columns of figures. For many purposes this definition is very good; for others, including our most serious purposes, it is no good at all. We are not likely to find out from such "experiments" how we should and can live together. As for the future, most of those who talk and write about it do so as if it already existed and as if we were being inexorably carried toward it, like passengers on a train moving toward a place they had not seen and could only wonder about. This is of course not true. The future does not exist. It has not been made. It is made only as we make it. The question we should be asking ourselves is what sort of future do we want. Part of my answer to that question is what I have written about in this book.

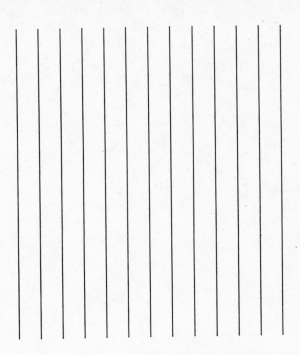

ESCAPE FROM CHILDHOOD

1. THE PROBLEM OF CHILDHOOD

This is a book about young people and their place, or lack of place, in modern society. It is about the *institution* of modern childhood, the attitudes, customs, and laws that define and locate children in modern life and determine to a large degree what their lives are like and how we, their elders, treat them. And it is about the many ways in which modern childhood seems to me to be bad for most of those who live within it and how it should and might be changed.

For a long time it never occurred to me to question this institution. Only in recent years did I begin to wonder whether there might be other or better ways for young people to live. By now I have come to feel that the fact of being a "child," of being wholly subservient and dependent, of being seen by older people as a mixture of expensive nuisance, slave, and super-pet, does most young people more harm than good.

I propose instead that the rights, privileges, duties, responsibilities of adult citizens be made *available* to any young person, of whatever age, who wants to make use of them. These would include, among others:

1. The right to equal treatment at the hands of the law —*i.e.,* the right, in any situation, to be treated no worse than an adult would be.

2. The right to vote, and take full part in political affairs.

3. The right to be legally responsible for one's life and acts.

4. The right to work, for money.

5. The right to privacy.

6. The right to financial independence and responsibility—*i.e.,* the right to own, buy, and sell property, to borrow money, establish credit, sign contracts, etc.

7. The right to direct and manage one's own education.

8. The right to travel, to live away from home, to choose or make one's own home.

9. The right to receive from the state whatever minimum income it may guarantee to adult citizens.

10. The right to make and enter into, on a basis of mutual consent, quasi-familial relationships outside one's

18

immediate family—*i.e.,* the right to seek and choose guardians other than one's own parents and to be legally dependent on them.

11. The right to do, in general, what any adult may legally do.

I have not tried to list these in any order of importance. What some young people might find most important others would find less so. I do not say, either, that these rights and duties should be tied into one package, that if a young person wants to assume any of them he must assume them all. He should be able to pick and choose. On the other hand, some of these rights are in the nature of things tied to others. Thus, the right to travel and to choose one's own home could hardly have much meaning to any young person who did not also have the right to legal and financial responsibility, to work, and to receive an income.

Some of these rights, much more than others, are linked to and depend on other kinds of change, in law, custom, or attitudes. Thus, we are likely to give young people of a given age—say, fourteen—the right to drive a car some time before we give them the right to vote, and we are likely to allow them to vote for some time before we give them the right to marry or to manage their own sex lives. And we are not likely to give young people the right to work at all in a society which, like the U.S. in 1973, tolerates massive unemployment and poverty. A country would have to make a political decision, like Sweden or Denmark, to do away with severe poverty and to maintain a high level of employment before adults would even consider allowing young people to compete for jobs. By the same token, no society is likely to give to young people the right to equal treatment before the law if it denies this right to adult women or to members of racial or other minority groups.

The changes I urge will certainly not come about all at once. If they take place, it will be as a process, a series of steps taken over a number of years. Thus, we have recently lowered the minimum voting age from twenty-one to eighteen. We should lower it still further, to sixteen or fifteen, and then later to fourteen or twelve, and so on, until this barrier, and all others that deny to young people the possibility of serious, independent, responsible participation in the life of the world around them, are done away with altogether. But this will take time. Perhaps it is best that it should.

A black woman, after hearing me discuss for a while at a meeting this question of modern childhood, asked me kindly but insistently why I took time to think or talk or write about this particular problem when all around me there were so many other obviously more serious and painful ones. Why not take first things first? She had in mind, of course, the problems of black people in America (and perhaps elsewhere). I write about this problem instead of others that also concern me, about the oppression of childhood rather than that of race, or sex, or age, or poverty, for several reasons. First, my concern and beliefs about it grow out of my own experience as a teacher, a student, and a friend of many childen. Secondly, I make myself—uninvited—a spokesman for children in this matter because they have so few other spokesmen and are in so poor a position to speak for themselves. Thirdly, I write hoping that those who may think of me as one who respects and cares about children may therefore listen somewhat more openly to what I say, however strange or frightening some of it may seem.

It is never easy to change old ideas and customs. Someone wrote of her grandmother that whenever she heard a new idea she responded in one of two ways: (1) it is crazy, or (2) I've always known it. The things we know and believe are a part of us. We feel we have always known them. Almost anything else, anything that doesn't fit into our structure of knowledge, our mental model of reality, is likely to seem strange, wild, fearful, dangerous, and impossible. People defend what they are used to even when it is hurting them. No one could be optimistic about the possibility of making the changes I propose in this book. How things will work out, no one can know. I can only say, *if* we are going to make a society and world in which people will be not only able to live but also glad to live, and in which the act of living will of itself make them more wise, responsible, and competent, *then* there are some things we must learn to do very differently.

Those who are skeptical about these changes may ask, "Even if we were to admit that the change you propose would bring about a better reality, can you prove that it would stay better? Might it not create problems and dangers and evils of its own?" The answer is yes, it would. No state of affairs is permanently perfect. Cures for old evils sooner or later create new ones. The most and best we can do is to try to change and cure what we know is wrong right now and deal with new evils as they come up. Of course, we have to try to use in the future as much of what we have learned in the past as we can. But though we can learn much from experience, we cannot learn everything. We can foresee and perhaps forestall some but not all of the problems that will arise in the future we make.

Like many others I used to think that people arrived at

truth through argument, debate, what some call "dialogue." These were kinds of trial by combat. Each person put his argument on a horse, so to speak, and ran him full tilt at the other person's argument. Whoever could knock the other off his horse won the combat, and the other had to say, "You win, you are right." But time and experience made it clear that people are not changed or won over by being made to see that their own ideas are foolish, illogical, or inconsistent. Now I have a vision—of the world as it is and as it may be— to share with any who may want to look at it. I can't plant this vision in their minds; everyone makes his own model of reality. But the light I throw on experience may help some of them to see things somewhat differently and to make a new vision of their own.

As I wrote earlier, it seems clear that if these changes take place they will do so in a number of steps, taken perhaps over many years. They are also not likely to take place except insofar as other kinds of social change have taken or are taking place. How great would such changes have to be? Some say very great. What I propose could well take place in any reasonably intelligent, honest, kindly, and humane country in which on the whole people do not need and crave power over others, do not worry much about being Number One, do not live under this constant threat of severe poverty, uselessness, and failure, do not exploit and prey upon each other. But it might take place even in countries that do not meet this description. The point is not to worry about what is possible but to do what we can.

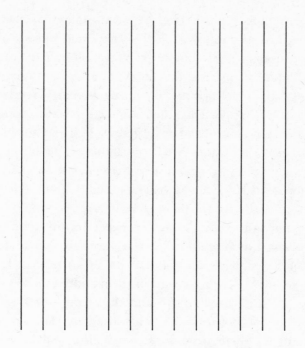

2. THE INSTITUTION OF CHILDHOOD

Of course, in one sense childhood is not an institution but a fact of human life. At birth we depend for our lives on others to take care of us, feed us, keep us warm and clean, and protect us from harm. In this we are like other animals. But unlike most animals, we do not outgrow our helplessness and dependency in a few months—it takes years. This is the fact of childhood, a fact as old as mankind. But it is also a fact that as we grow older we do continue to get more able to take care of ourselves.

When I was first teaching school in Colorado there came

to the school for a while twin boys from Italy. An American who lived up the valley from the school had some years before heard about these boys when traveling in Italy and had made himself their foster parent. When they were very small, at most four or five years old, during World War II, their parents had disappeared—killed or taken prisoner. Somehow these two small boys had managed to live and survive for several years, in a large city, in a country terribly torn and dislocated by war, in the midst of great poverty and privation —*all by themselves*. They had apparently found or made some sort of shelter for themselves in a graveyard and lived by begging and stealing what they needed. Only after several years of this life were they discovered and brought under the wing of the state. They were living in an orphan asylum when the American first heard of them and began to take an interest in their growing up and their education. He sent them to our school for a while because he thought it would be useful for them to know some English and hoped that they might learn it there.

I don't want to be understood as saying that I think it is good for small children to live alone in graveyards, or even that the response of these two boys to this experience was typical. But the fact remains that they did not seem to have been deeply or permanently hurt by that experience. Though smaller for their age than most Americans, they were exceedingly quick, strong, and well coordinated, by far the best soccer players in the school. Also, though they were not very good students and not much interested in learning English—what good would it do them back in Bologna?— they were friendly, lively, curious, enthusiastic, and, in spite of the language barrier, much liked by all who knew them at school. Clearly it may be possible for us to outgrow our phys-

24

ical helplessness and dependency much sooner or faster than most people think.

We might think of human life as a sort of curve, starting at birth, rising to various peaks of physical, mental, and social power, continuing for some time on a kind of plateau, and then slowly declining to old age and death. This curve of life is different for all human beings. Sometimes it is cut abruptly short by death. But for every human being that curve is a single curve, a wholeness. It is of course a curve of continual growth and change. To some degree we are different every day from what we were the day before. But this growth and change are continuous. There are no breaks or gaps in it. We do not, like some insects, suddenly turn from one kind of creature into another that is very different.

Here the fact of childhood ends and the institution of childhood begins. Childhood as we now know it has divided that curve of life, that wholeness, into two parts—one called Childhood, the other called Adulthood, or Maturity. It has made a Great Divide in human life, and made us think that the people on opposite sides of this divide, the Children and the Adults, are very different. Thus we *act* as if the differences between any sixteen-year-old and any twenty-two-year-old were far greater and more important than the differences between someone aged two and someone aged sixteen, or between someone aged twenty-two and someone aged seventy. For with respect to the kind of control he has over his own life, the ability to make important choices, the sixteen-year-old is much closer to the two-year-old than he is to someone of twenty-two.

In short, by the institution of childhood I mean all those attitudes and feelings, and also customs and laws, that put a great gulf or barrier between the young and their elders, and the world of their elders; that make it difficult or impossible for young people to make contact with the larger society around them, and, even more, to play any kind of active, responsible, useful part in it; that lock the young into eighteen years or more of subserviency and dependency, and make of them, as I said before, a mixture of expensive nuisance, fragile treasure, slave, and super-pet.

For a while I thought of calling this book *The Prison of Childhood* or, as other friends suggested, using the word "Liberation" in the title. But one friend objected that *The Prison of Childhood* made it sound as if everyone who supported the present institution of childhood did so because he disliked children and wanted to keep them in some sort of prison. This, she insisted, is not so. Many people who believe in our present ways of raising children, and who will therefore deeply dislike many or most of the ideas in this book, are people who like children and want to do what they think is best for them.

I agreed and gave up both "Prison" and "Liberation," both of which imply letting children out of a bad place that bad people have locked them into. The word "escape" need not imply this. If we are in a house that catches fire, or on a boat that begins to sink, we want to escape—but this does not mean that we think someone lured or put us into that house or boat. Also, "escape" is a word of action. To escape from a danger, you must first decide that it *is* a danger and then act to get away from it. I want to leave to the young the right to make that decision and to choose and take that action.

Most people who believe in the institution of childhood as we know it see it as a kind of walled garden in which children, being small and weak, are protected from the harshness of the world outside until they become strong and clever enough to cope with it. Some children experience childhood in just that way. I do not want to destroy their garden or kick them out of it. If they like it, by all means let them stay in it. But I believe that most young people, and at earlier and earlier ages, begin to experience childhood not as a garden but as a prison. What I want to do is put a gate, or gates, into the wall of the garden, so that those who find it no longer protective or helpful, but instead confining and humiliating, can move out of it and for a while try living in a larger space. If that proves too much for them, they can always come back into the garden. Indeed, perhaps we all ought to have walled gardens to take refuge in when we feel we must.

I am not saying that childhood is bad for all children all the time. But Childhood, as in Happy, Safe, Protected, Innocent Childhood, does not exist for many children. For many other children, however good it may be, childhood goes on far too long, and there is no gradual, sensible, and painless way to grow out of it or leave it.

Some children have no families. Their parents are dead or have abandoned them. Or the law may have taken them from their parents, perhaps because they brutalized or neglected them, perhaps because the state did not approve of their parents' politics or morals or style of life. Most children who lose their families remain wards of the state—*i.e.,* they are prisoners. That is the choice the law now offers. If you can't (or won't) be a child, you must be a convict, in some kind of jail, guarded by people whose chief concern is to keep you from running away.

Many children live seemingly normal lives in seemingly normal families. But their childhood, if in some respects safe, is by no means happy, protected, or innocent. On the contrary, they may be in many ways exploited, bullied, humiliated, and mistreated by their families. But even in such families life might not be so painful and destructive for the young if they could now and then get away for a while from parents, or rival brothers and sisters.

For many children, childhood, happy and ideal though it may be, simply goes on too long. Among families that I know well, many children who for years have been living happily with their parents have suddenly found them intolerable and have become intolerable to them. The happier was their previous life together, the more painful will this be for the parents, and perhaps for the young person as well. "We used to get along so well." "He used to be so happy." "I don't know what's gotten into him." "We must have done something wrong, but we can't imagine what it is." Many times, too, I have heard a young person, usually in late teens or early twenties, say, "I love my parents, we've always gotten along very well, but now they want me to do this, or that, and I don't want to do it, I want to do something else, which they don't like. I feel so guilty and confused, I don't know what to do. I don't want to hurt them but I have to live my own life." The end of childhood seems often most painful for those whose childhood was most happy.

It goes on too long, and there is too seldom any sensible and gradual way to move out of it and into a different life, a different relationship with the parents. When the child can find no way to untie the bonds to his parents, the only thing left for him is to break them. The stronger the bonds, the harder and more desperate must be the pull required to break them. This can cause terrible, almost unforgettable bad feelings, injury, and pain. It is as if, having no other way to get out of the nest, the young had no choice but to blow it up.

A sign in a Boston subway says NO ONE EVER RUNS AWAY FROM A HAPPY HOME. But the happiest homes may give to the children just that extra confidence, curiosity, and energy that makes them want to test their strength and skill against a larger world. If they are then not allowed to do it—that's when the unhappiness starts.

Not long ago I was asked to speak at a number of meetings in schools in a lower-middle-class near-suburb of a midwestern city. Almost everyone worked either as fairly well-paid union labor in large industries or in lower-level white collar jobs. Most of the adults were the children or grandchildren of immigrants and wanted very much for their children to go to college and establish themselves firmly in the middle class. By conventional standards the politics of the district are well over to the right.

It had been arranged that during the afternoon, in one of the junior high schools, I was to spend a class period in a joint meeting of two ninth grade English classes, discussing with the students whatever they and I wanted to talk about. It had also been agreed that at this meeting I would be the only adult in the group, but for some reason a number of the school officials who had been showing me around followed me into the classroom. The appearance of these well-known authority figures ended our chances for any very free or candid discussion. A few students, either fearless by nature, or so successful that they did not have to worry about getting in trouble, or in so much trouble already that they did not have to worry about getting into any more, did almost all of what little talking was done.

I had been talking about schools and school reform. In

the closing minutes of the period, it occurred to me to try to find out what some of these young people thought about the institution of childhood. And let me stress again, these were not radical or even liberal young people. The local high school had only just modified, and very slightly, its dress code. In this junior high school, the boys had to wear coats and ties; the girls, dresses or skirts. They were running a tight ship in this school, and most of the top brass was right there in the room.

I asked three questions, for a show-of-hands response. The first was, "If you could legally vote in political elections, how many of you think that at least some of the time you would vote?" About two-thirds of the students raised their hands, many of them slowly and thoughtfully. The second was, "If you could legally work for money, how many of you think that at least some of the time you would work?" Again, about two-thirds raised their hands. One boy in the front row, who had not spoken during the discussion, said, "Hey, we're going to have to spend the rest of our lives working, what's the big hurry to start?" People laughed, but the hands stayed up. Finally, almost as an afterthought, not expecting any particular response, I asked the third question: "If you could legally live away from home, how many of you think that at least some of the time you would do so?" Every hand shot into the air, so quickly and violently that I half expected shoulders to pop out of joint. Faces came alive. Clearly, I had touched a magic button. I thought to myself, "If only I had thought to ask that sooner, how much I might have learned." But the period was at an end. I thanked the students, wished them luck, and they filed out of the room. My hosts and I continued our tour of the schools. No one mentioned that last response, and I thought it better to let it drop.

Some might say that the young people only wanted to get away from home and the nay-saying parents so that they could enjoy forbidden adult pleasures—smoking, drinking, sex—but though this may be part of what those young people were saying, I think that they were also saying that they want to live, at least for a while, among other people who might see them and deal with them as people, not as children.

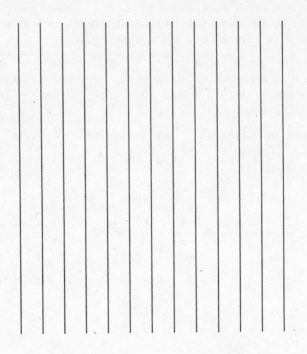

3. CHILDHOOD IN HISTORY

To defend and justify the institution of childhood we make idealized pictures of family life which often have little to do with reality. The other day an old friend of mine, in whose family I have spent much time, and whose children I have seen grow up, told me about a talk she had with two of her children. Dinner at her house is always a happy, talkative occasion. Not long ago she and the two children were watching an episode on the TV show "An American Family." Discussing it with them later, she said she found the film artificial—who could imagine a family sitting around a dinner table and eating a whole meal without talking? The two children insisted she was wrong. "How many times do I have to tell you," the older one said, "that when I go out to dinner at my friends' houses no one says *anything*—except maybe to pass this or that, or 'use your napkin.' *We* are the only ones who sit around and talk all the time." The younger child said that when *he* goes out to dinner at his friends' houses, usually they don't even sit around a table, just kind of stand around in the kitchen and grab whatever food is at hand.

This talk brought back a memory. In the summer of 1956 I took a group of ten young Americans on a trip to France, under the Experiment in International Living. For a month we lived, each with a different French family, in the small town of Gap, in southeastern France. At the end of the summer, coming home on a student ship, we talked about our experiences. I asked my companions what had impressed them most of all the things they had seen and done, what did they most want to bring back with them and make a part of their lives. Almost all of them said, "We like the daily family dinner, all the family coming together, young and old and in between, with plenty of time for leisurely talk, a chance for everyone to have his say, no one left out." They spoke with surprising nostalgia, longing, and regret. Without exception, these otherwise typical young Americans told me that in their families, and in all the families they knew, such family meals hardly ever took place—only at Christmas, Thanksgiving, and such special occasions. Most of the time everyone was too busy with his own affairs. People came in at odd hours, grabbed a bite out of the icebox or off the stove, left a message or two about where they were going, and went on their way again.

Perhaps, when a custom, a ritual, a tradition, an institution seems most to need preserving, it is already past preserving, has lost most of its life. Perhaps the modern family was already largely dead well before anyone began publicly to attack or defend it. We do not defend furiously what has most real value in our lives; it seems as natural and inevitable as breathing. What we defend most hotly are those things we think we ought to value but secretly know or fear we do not. It is only when our institutions (like our bodies) become seriously ill that we stop taking their health for granted.

Those who have recently begun to study the origins and history of childhood appear to have learned that childhood, motherhood, home, family, all of these institutions as we know them, are in important respects local and recent inventions, not some universal part of the human condition.

In *The Dialectics of Sex,* Shulamith Firestone points out:

> After the fourteenth century, with the development of the bourgeoisie and empirical science, this situation slowly began to evolve. The concept of childhood developed as an adjunct to the modern family . . . "childrenese" became fashionable during the seventeenth century . . . Children's toys did not appear until 1600 and even then were not used beyond the age of three or four. . . . But by the late seventeenth century special artifacts for children were common. Also in the late seventeenth century we find the introduction of special children's games . . . *childhood did not apply to women.* The female child went from swaddling clothes right into adult female dress. She did not go to school, which, as we shall see, was the institution that structured childhood. At the age of nine or ten she acted, literally, like a "little lady"; her activity did not differ from that of adult

women. As soon as she reached puberty, as early as ten or twelve, she was married off to a much older male.

Aries quotes Heroard, *Journal sur L'enfance et la Jeunesse de Louis XIII,* the detailed account of the Dauphin's childhood years written by his doctor, to the effect that the Dauphin sang and played the violin at the age of seventeen months. He goes on to say that at the same age the child played a game called Mall, something like golf, or perhaps croquet; he talked; and he played games of military strategy. At three and four respectively, he learned to read and write. At four and five the Dauphin, though still playing with dolls, practiced archery and played cards and chess. Five-year-olds I have known have tended to resist the rigidity of the rules of a game and to want to change them when they are losing. But the Dauphin was perhaps more used to games. And I once played checkers with a boy of about six who prepared a triple-jump trap for me, which I would have fallen into had I not noticed that he was looking at me with a peculiar intentness and excitement. We are told that from the time he was able to walk, the Dauphin mixed with adults as an equal in all their activities, dancing, acting, and taking part in all their amusements. Of course, we don't know how well he did any of these things. Being a future king no doubt gave him certain advantages. No doubt the older people made more generous allowances for his lack of skill than they might have been willing to make to children of lesser rank. But this misses the essential point, that adults of that time felt that the way they *ought* to behave to a young prince was to treat him as much like themselves as possible.

Not only is childhood as we know it a modern invention, but so is the family we talk so much about preserving. In *Man's World, Woman's Place,* Elizabeth Janeway writes, in part:

> What Aries' book suggests (and it is not the only one to do so) is that our idea of a "home" centered on one tightly knit group of parents and children denotes a way of living that did not last very long historically, or spread very wide geographically. . . . More and more the group that made up a household became the "nuclear family" of parents and children, living together in privacy and increasingly cut off from the wider community life of earlier times and regions other than Northern Europe. Servants now formed a separate subordinate class, working within the house for the comfort of those living there instead of as apprentices or journeymen manufacturing goods for consumption or market. *House* was becoming *home* by separating itself from the world of work and turning into a stronghold of family living and leisure. [P. 14]
>
> Before 1700, except in very rare instances [the myth of home, hearth, and children] didn't exist at all—there were no homes in our sense for women to be in.
>
> Where were women, then, if they were not at home? If family-centered life is an invention of the middle class, how did people live in earlier times? . . . They lived in one or the other of two kinds of dwellings: the big house or the hovel. . . . In the big houses dwelt the elite, but not alone in their domestic circle, for the big houses were not merely places to live. They were fortresses, or economic centers, or both. Within their gates, the family was surrounded by servants, apprentices, employees of all levels, bailiffs and managers, clerks and clerics, and countless visitors and hangers-on. All told, about 20 percent of the population lived in such quarters, masters and servants cheek by jowl, in rooms . . . where no one was ever alone.

The rest of the population lived in the little houses, city or country. They were quite simply, slums. [P. 15]

Children were in adult life partly because there was no way to keep them out. Poor people, of course, had then as now so little space in which to live that children had to see and know about all the realities of life. But even in the houses of the wealthiest people there was none of the privacy we now think so important. The houses, even palatial castles, did not have private rooms leading off a common hall. The rooms were in rows, one leading to the next, so that to get from one room to a more distant one you had to go through all the rooms in between. Everyone saw, could not help seeing, all the things that other people were doing. The natural functions of life were not taboo as they later became.

Even motherhood itself is not the enduring and universal relationship and need that we have taken it to be. Ms. Janeway writes:

We might remember, I think, that mothers did work hard in the past and certainly did not spend all their time with their families. Millions of children, in fact, through century after century, have been raised in large part by women who were not their natural mothers. I do not mean only the children of the kibbutzim, but all those babies put out to nurse, left with grandmothers or older sisters, and sent away to school (or, earlier, to the great houses) when they reached the age of reason, an age which is and has been thought of around the world with considerable uniformity as being about seven years old. In our own cultural past (that is, in medieval Europe), when the only formal schools which existed were devoted to training boys for the church, the rest of the folk, noble, gentle, or serf, learned by doing in a kind of general apprenticeship to the adult world, and

37

they learned a lot of it a lot of the time away from home. Even when formal education came to be thought of as desirable for the laity and upper-class boys were sent to school, girls and boys from the lower classes continued to learn in the old-fashioned way; it was only the daughters of the rich and great who were kept at home with a governness. The rest learned by working sometimes with their own parents, who were not necessarily more tender than strangers, but very frequently while boarding with friends or relations or in the home of some well-placed notable, to learn manners as well as crafts.

No doubt, one may say, this happened. But were these arrangements good for the children? How can one answer—except to say that the human race survived them as it has other ways of life that seem strange today, and that the customs themselves must have been socially useful and psychologically satisfactory enough to endure. [P. 187]

Paul Murray Kendall in his biography *Richard III* writes at one point that an Italian visitor to England was shocked to find that it was the custom of all rich and noble families to send their children away from home at the age of about eight or nine, to live until they were adults in other people's households, where they worked as servants, waited on tables, and learned various arts and skills. Indeed, these children never did return home, at least not to live. The sons made their own lives, and the marriages of the daughters were arranged by the families with whom they were living.

I do not claim that young people were happier before modern childhood was invented, or that in some ways it did not improve the lives of some children, or that even now it is always and everywhere bad for everybody. All I am saying is this, that it doesn't work well for many people, and that those people for whom it doesn't work ought to be allowed to try something else.

Nor do I claim that modern childhood is bad simply because it is new, or that it is in every way a radical departure from previous ways of dealing with children. Children for as far back as we know have always been owned and controlled by adults. What is both new and bad about modern childhood is that children are so cut off from the adult world. Children have always been bossed around by their parents. What is new is being bossed around *only* by their parents, having almost no contact with adults *except* their parents.

The older way of dealing with children, of considering them as part of the adult world, was not something carefully planned and thought out. It grew out of the natural conditions of life. For one thing, in any society where there is always more to do than people to do it, children will naturally be expected to help as soon and as much as they can; and when they are still too small to help, there will not be any special people around who have nothing to do but look after them. We constantly ask ourselves, in anxiety and pain, "What is best for the children, what is right for the children, what should we do for the children?" The question is an effect as well as a cause of modern childhood. Until the institution was invented, it would hardly have occurred to anyone to ask the question or, if they had, to suppose that what was good for children was any different from what was good for everyone else.

J. H. van den Berg, in *The Changing Nature of Man,* uses often and in many ways the metaphor of distance. The adult removes himself from the child, he pushes the child away, the adult and child are standing on opposite sides of a gulf that grows wider. Many things contributed to the making of that gulf. To some extent the adults created it deliberately, perhaps in part because of the influence of Rousseau, who loudly proclaimed that the child was a very different creature and had to be treated differently. They removed the child from their world (or their world from him) because they thought it would be better for him. But to a much larger extent the world removed itself from children (and adults as well) as it became more and more abstract and opaque, as it became harder and harder for anyone to see or know what was going on, or who was doing what, or why.

One of the things that helped remove the world from children was a change in the nature of work. Throughout most of the life of man, much of his work has been hard, arduous, even exhausting, and often also dangerous. But much of it required strength, skill, and judgment; much of it was work he was proud to do, and to do well; and hardly any of it seemed pointless. People had not become alienated or separated from their work. They knew what they were doing and why. Also, they did most of it in or close to their homes. But with increasing specialization, industrialization, and centralization, work became more remote and more meaningless and hateful. More and more adults did it where children could not see them do it, or understand it if they did. More and more adults did not want children to do the work they did and, indeed, often did not want to do it themselves.

Ms. Janeway writes:

. . . how [computer programmers do their work] is, for laymen, occult knowledge. This is not a matter of well-preserved "craft mysteries" as it was in the past, but simply a result of the distance that exists today between one section of life and another. [P. 78]

Here is the metaphor of distance again. It is common, because true, to say that life today is fragmented, that the parts of life have become separated from each other. Ms. Janeway says that personal roles seem vital to people because they are the only ones they understand and feel sure of. Thus they might say, "I don't know what I'm doing most the time, but I do know what I'm doing when I'm being a father or a mother." Elsewhere she points out that it is precisely those women who feel least in control of their own lives who have most need to control the lives of their children.

But it is because society has become so complicated, because adults act in such a variety of ways, because people seem to be playing so many different roles, because there are so many different ways of living and working that young people need to have access to more rather than fewer older people as they grow up. In a simple and stable society, any one person is more likely to be typical of most people than in a larger and more complicated one. In a simple society it might be true that to understand what one's father does at home and work is to understand a lot about what all fathers do. But this is not true in a society as complicated and varied as ours.

The world, and life in the world, have meaning when most people understand the ways in which most human needs are met; it loses meaning when they are no longer able to. In Mexico, even in fairly prosperous and modern towns, most new buildings are built in the same way, a post-and-beam construction of reinforced concrete with the walls filled in with brick and/or windows. Anyone watching people build such a building can fairly soon understand all the parts of the process and can very quickly learn to take part in it and help do it. Any young person who grows up there knows how houses and buildings are built and knows it would be easy to build or learn to build one oneself. Not so, however, with the great skyscrapers of modern (including Mexican) cities. There, even of the people working, only a few know what is going on. The spectators on the sidewalk are watching a mystery. They feel, and perhaps rightly, that it would take most of a lifetime to understand the process before them. And the same is true, for most people, of everything they see and use in their lives.

But, says van den Berg, there is a more fundamental reason for the distance that opened up between the child and the adult, and the adult and his world. It has to do with the way we look at things. Much of the meaning of man's world was destroyed, at least for most men, when his philosophers invented causality. For this invention put the meaning of present reality into the past, a past which itself became increasingly unknowable and meaningless as human life changed ever more rapidly. The principle of causality tells us that everything that happens is the result of, and therefore caused by and *determined by,* something that happened before. The child asks, why is the fire burning? Because someone lit it with a match. Why did the match burn? Because someone scratched it against the box. Why did that make it burn? Because there was a chemical on the end of the match and something else on the box. Why was the chemical on the end of the match? Because someone dipped it into . . . Back, back, back, into time. Van den Berg tells of a poignant incident in which his eight-year-old asked him why the leaves on the trees were turning red. He wanted to know like all children what was the purpose of this, the point of it. But his father led him instead into a maze of meaningless biology and chemistry, knowing that he was moving away from the child and his question and concerns, but because of his scientific training unable to stop himself. The child wanted to know the point of what he could see around him, but could get no answer. For if everything is the result of something in the past, *nothing has any point.*

People used to see the meaning of life in terms of purpose. In a short-run and immediate sense, they knew, could see the purpose of what was going on around them. The answer to the child's question "Why is that happening?" did not lie in the past. It was not, because something happened yesterday, that happened because something happened the day before yesterday, and so on. It was, so that something else can happen. That man is cutting down that tree to make boards to make a house to live in or to make a fire to cook his dinner. That man is cutting that piece of leather so that he can make a shoe out of it so that someone can put it on his foot and not hurt it when he walks on rough ground. And in a larger sense the world and life had a purpose too, though it was God's purpose, and ordinary people did not know and were not encouraged to know very much about it.

All of this we have destroyed, everything has a cause, nothing has a meaning, the universe is a machine set mysteriously into motion a long time ago and slowly running down, and we are little machines running down in it. Meanwhile the world around us changes ever faster, so that the past itself disappears, loses its significance. Margaret Mead said not long ago that today the young know much more about the world in many ways than their elders. The world the old people knew about, spent much of their lives learning about, has already disappeared. But it is in many ways a terrible thing to grow up in a world in which your grandparents must ask *you* questions to find out what is going on.

How are we to put back in our world a sense of stability and human and humane purpose? Until we do, the world will not regain its meaning for us, and all of us, young and old alike, will remain bewildered and lost.

4. THE FAMILY AND ITS PURPOSES

Some fear that giving or offering children the right to greater independence will threaten or weaken or destroy "the institution of the family." But the family of which most people speak now—Mom, Pop, and the kids—is a modern invention. The family even as most people knew it in this country a hundred years ago has been almost entirely destroyed, mostly by the automobile and the restless and rootless society it has helped to create. That family was in turn very different from the European family of three hundred years before, when the whole notion of the home and the family as private had not yet been invented. In any case there is much evidence that the modern nuclear family is not only the source of many people's most severe problems but also is breaking down in many ways or changing into new forms.

Whatever is strong and healthy in families, whatever meets real human needs, enhances and enriches life, cannot and will not be threatened by what I propose here. Any institution that really works is immune to attack, however severe. Reality has its own strength. People with genuinely strong religious beliefs are not threatened by talk that God does not exist or is dead. Happily married couples who after many years get great strength and joy from each other's company simply smile and go on with their life when they hear that marriage is nothing but a device for the exploitation of women, or whatever it may be. Their experience tells them better.

At its very best, the family can be what many people say it is, an island of acceptance and love in the midst of a harsh world. But too often within the family people take out on each other all the pain and frustrations of their lives that they don't dare take out on anyone else. Instead of a ready-made source of friends, it is too often a ready-made source of victims and enemies, the place where not the kindest but the cruelest words are spoken.

This may disappoint us, but it should not surprise or horrify us. The family was not invented, nor has it evolved, to make children happy or to provide a secure emotional and psychological background to grow up in. Mankind evolved the family to meet a very basic need in small and precarious societies—to make sure that as many children as possible were born and, once born, physically taken care of until they could take care of themselves. "Be fruitful and multiply," commanded the Bible. A society or community that did not was sure to be wiped out, by drought, famine, plague, or war. The rulers of these societies solved their problem in a way that is the foundation of our moral codes today, though these codes now do not meet, but oppose, our most urgent survival needs. What they did was to harness the sexual drives of young men to the begetting and nurturing of young children. The rules boiled down to this. You can't have sex except to make a baby; you have to take care of the woman who will be the baby's mother; and when the baby is born you have to take care of it as well. This was a burden, heavy then as now, which most young men would have avoided if they could. But loopholes were tightly closed, the rules strictly forbade getting sexual release or pleasure in any other way. And society sweetened the deal a little bit. In return for the trouble of taking care of this woman and her child or children, society gave them to the man as his property. They had to work for him and do what he told them. Since human energy was both a scarce resource and a valuable form of capital, a man with a large family was generally felt to be rich and fortunate. The invention worked, and the people multiplied. How they did multiply! In short, the family was an institution in which some people were owned by others. Men owned women, and male and female children learned to own and be owned.

If the family became other things besides, as it often did, it was because people who live close together for a long time have to find some way to make this somewhat palatable and workable and because man is a social and affectionate creature who, with any luck, will become fond of many of the people he is closest to. But the family was not invented to give people someone to love. To the extent that came, it was extra. Basically the family was and is a tiny kingdom, an absolute monarchy. Roman law gave the father the right to life and death over his wife and children, as over his slaves. Fathers in some Arab countries have rights close to this even today. Within the past months a father in one Arab country, who had killed his fifteen-year-old daughter because she was too friendly with the boys—there was no charge that she was having sexual relations with them—and who had spent seven months in prison for doing this, was granted full pardon by the head of state, a very popular decision. Within the past few weeks I have read accounts in major newspapers and magazines of parents kidnapping their children, often well into their twenties, and keeping them prisoner, often for weeks, in order to free them from the "influence" of certain religious communities. Nobody suggests that in such cases our otherwise rather severe laws against kidnapping should apply. Apparently kidnapping is okay if it is your own kid— no matter how old he is.

It is the family in this sense that is most heatedly defended. Most of those people who talk angrily about saving the family or bringing back the virtues of the family do not see it as an instrument of growth and freedom but of dominance and slavery, a miniature dictatorship (sometimes justified by "love") in which the child learns to live under and submit to absolute and unquestionable power. It is a training for slavery.

Others, more kindly, insist that only in the family can children grow up healthy. Elizabeth Janeway puts it thus:

> . . . Children do indeed need to be brought up, and brought up in intimate, familiar surroundings. They need love, stability, consistent and unequivocal care and lasting relation-

ships with people who are profoundly enough interested in them to look after them with warmth, gaiety, and patience.

This notion that a child cannot grow up healthy unless he is at every moment under the eye of some adult who has nothing to do but watch over him is very modern.

And Ms. Janeway, in other parts of her book, shows over and over again that most children never had the kind of care modern dogma says they must have. Thus on page 180:

. . . Most women who work do so because they need the money. They work at unglamorous jobs, not at careers—and they always have.

This suggests something interesting about the context of our mythic statement that woman's place is in the home. We have seen that, as far as history goes, it is very much a middle-class myth. . . . The myth as we know it reflects a society that can afford to hold women off the labor market and keep them at home in a more or less Veblenesque situation.

Another modern idea is that children get from the family their models of grown-up life, their ideas of what it is to be a man or a woman. Ms. Janeway quotes the sociologist Talcott Parsons as saying that "children learn about the world and the culture in which they live by growing up in the subdivision of that culture which we call the nuclear family. . . . Later he learns that the members of his family represent social relationships that are common to the rest of the world he lives in." Today, it is hard to find much truth in this. And what need had children of such "models" when the life of the adults went on all around them, in full view, when they lived their own lives in the middle of that adult life, when they joined the adults often in work, play, ceremony, festival, death, mourning? And what kind of model of adult life does the modern child get, who sees his father come home in the evening, sit down, perhaps read the paper, and spend the rest of the evening and much of the weekend watching television, or who sees the mother doing household chores. Is this, then, all that men and women do? Not only is the modern nuclear family a very bad model of adult and social life, because so incomplete and distorted, but it is its isolation from the world that creates the need for models.

For many reasons children need a much larger network of people to relate to. The small family is so often unhelpful or destructive because it is so small. The relationships are too intense, too much is always at stake. Many parents find it hard to say no to their children even though they say it much too often, because it seems to threaten their ideal relationship with the child. They have to get angry before they can say no, and then they are doubly angry at the child for "making" them say no. The family is so dependent on these high-powered feelings, so shut in on itself, so non-involved with others or with the community, so devoid of purposes outside of itself, that it is fragile, easily threatened by a quarrel. Human relations cannot be only about human relations. If there is nothing in a family but feelings, if it is only an arena for feelings, if its life depends on everyone feeling good about or loving everyone else, if the members have no other way of being really useful to each other, then it is constantly threatened by anything that might upset the good feelings, and perfectly normal differences and quarrels take on too much importance.

I occasionally say no to a seven-year-old friend of mine

(as she occasionally says it to me). When I do, I say it without having to think, how will she feel about me tomorrow, or have I been saying no too often, or will this hurt our friendship. Because I don't worry, she doesn't have to worry. The no is a thing of the moment, connected only with the act of the moment. It is not part of a larger yes or no about her as a person. So she takes the no for what it is, and life moves on. We continue to know each other as growing and changing people, getting and giving what knowledge or pleasure we can but not wholly dependent on each other and hence not wholly vulnerable.

A pat phrase of our time is "sibling rivalry." We take as healthy and right what is only "normal" in the sense that it is all too common—that the children in a family should actively dislike each other and compete frantically and ruthlessly for the too scarce attention and "love" of their parents. Why should the competition be so frantic? Because the wanted and needed attention, concern, advice, companionship, and protection are so scarce. Why so scarce? Because there is no one but the parents to give it.

Children need many more adult friends, people with whom they may have more easy relationships that they can easily move out of or away from whenever they need to or feel like it. Perhaps they found many of these in extended families, among various grandparents, aunts, uncles, cousins, in-laws, and so on. Perhaps they found them living in smaller communities, villages, or towns, or neighborhoods in larger cities. But these communities, in which people have a sense of place and mutual concern, are more rare all the time, disappearing from country as well as city. The extended family has been scattered by the automobile and the airplane. There is no way to bring it together so that children may live close to numbers of older people who will in some degree have an interest in them and care about them.

What we need is to re-create the extended family. Or rather, we need to allow, encourage, and help young people create extended families of their own. There is no reason why the adult friends of a child should be friends of his parents. Parents generally want friends like themselves. Children may like more variety so that they may get some things from one person and some things from another. During my sister's growing up one of her closest friends, and one very important to her, was an older woman that our parents hardly knew and might well not have liked. Many young people in their twenties and thirties are now trying to re-create the lost extended family or community in organizations of one kind or another. These are often good for them but may be less good for their children, if only because the people who live in these communes tend to be too much alike. And there is no reason why the network of people with whom we, or children, are most closely linked—what Vonnegut in *Cat's Cradle* called a *karass*—should all have to live close to us.

Robert Frost, in his poem "Death of the Hired Man," put it very well. The hired man, now too old and ill to work, is sitting exhausted in the kitchen of a younger farm couple. The husband, not quite knowing what to do about him or with him, wonders why he has come to their house, since he has other relatives nearby. For answer his wife says to him— it could not be said better—"Home is where, when you have to go there, they have to let you in."

Just so. Children need many such homes. Perhaps we all do. But I think many adults, much more than children, have a sense of having many homes, places where in time of bad need or trouble we could go and be sure of getting help, or at least shelter. But the making and finding of these homes is not, on the whole, something that society can do for people. Each person as he lives must find and make his own. This is what I want to allow and help children to do.

5. ON THE LOSS OF AUTHORITY
OF THE OLD

We talk a great deal these days, as perhaps people always have, about how and why the older generation has lost its authority over the young. Most of the people who ask that question say that the older generation lost its authority by being too easy, too soft, by letting the young do too much of what they wanted, by not making them afraid. But we know that many of our most unruly young, in or out of schools, the ones who most fiercely and violently defy all authority, who form gangs and commit crimes, are those who in their early years were most strictly and punitively brought up.

An important part of the answer lies elsewhere. Whenever I hear talk about the loss of authority of the older generation, I think of something that happened in my fifth grade classroom in about 1959. At a time during the day when the children were free to move around the room and talk, I overheard one of them in a group of four or five say to the others, "If I grow up . . ." What was this talk? "If I grow up." Knowing ten-year-olds, how challenging and sassy they are, how quick to pick up on anything they think is silly or out of place, I expected one of the others to say something like, "What do you mean, 'If I grow up?' Are you sick, or something?" But no one interrupted. After a while I realized that the speaker had spoken for all of them.

It was as if the ground had opened up under my feet. "If I grow up." I could remember a little of my own life at ten. I had my share of worries, problems, fears. But they certainly did not include any worry as to whether I might or might not grow up. Of course I was going to grow up. I had only the vaguest sense of the future; my imagination and ambition could take me no further than the hope that someday I might play on a college football team. Beyond that, I had no idea. The future was no clearer six years later. But I was at least sure that I would have a future. Life was out there in front of me.

A few other things my fifth-graders said or wrote made it clear that most of them, all upper-middle class to wealthy, did not have any very secure sense of the future, of a life waiting for them. Some years later I read that many young people of this age group—they were among the ones who had to practice hiding under their school desks in atomic bomb drills—reported to psychologists or psychiatrists that they had frequent nightmares about atomic war, the end of the world, and so on. I had spent far more time thinking about the bomb and what to do about it than many of these young people had or would. But not once, then or since, have I ever had a dream about atomic war or the end of the world. At the deepest levels of my being, for no reason, I assume that the bomb will not go off. A great many young people believe that it will. As a child, happy or unhappy, I was certain that there was a future ahead for me. My fifth grade students, who with others of their age were ten years later to become the most unruly of all college generations, were not. Often I have read about people who, asking young people why they smoked in spite of clear evidence that it would shorten their lives, were told by them that they didn't expect to live past forty anyway. I think it was Lewis Mumford who said of many of the young people he has talked to that in their minds and hearts they lived in the aftermath, the shattered wreckage, of a third World War—as if the worst that we could imagine *had already happened.* Such feelings are strong in much of what younger people, in their books, news-papers, and magazines, now write.

Surely this feeling has much to do with the loss of au-thority of the old. Authority is never based *only* on force. An authority that can only depend on force is already dead and will soon disappear. True authority may now and then ex-press itself in force, as a reminder or to control some excep-tional outsiders. But if it is true and legitimate its base is moral. Ours is probably not the first culture in which the young have struggled to assert themselves against their elders, the elders in turn struggling to push them back, saying, not yet, not yet. But in earlier cultures the young knew that the elders held the key to the future. They were running a so-ciety, a way of life, a going concern; and when they felt the young were ready, they would turn it over to them. And so, when the elders said, do it our way, trust us, we know and you do not, you are not ready yet, at least something in the minds or hearts of the young would respond with, perhaps they're right, we'll get our turn, maybe these old guys do know, at least some of the time, what they are doing.

But when ten-year-olds in the most favored families in the most favored nation in the world cannot look forward with any assurance even to growing up, we do not have any longer a world in which one can say that Daddy Knows Best.

Children are sensitive to faces. Like all slaves, all power-less people, they learn to look at and read the faces of their rulers in order to sense what will or may happen next. They are good at reading faces. What they see on many of them must make them very uneasy. Erich Fromm wrote some-where of seeing in a leading picture magazine a photo of a group of people standing at a street corner in a large city. The photographer had used a long telephoto lens, so that the people did not know they were being photographed. On the faces of most of them were expressions of such horror, pain, fear, and disgust that Fromm at first assumed they had just seen a dreadful accident. But no—they were simply standing waiting for a green light. The voices are often no better, the laughter often worst of all. How could one trust or want to be like people who look and sound like that?

A generation that does not believe it can make a future that it will like, or trust or love any future it can imagine, has nothing to pass on to and hence nothing to say to the young. It might seem a paradox that our society, which per-haps more than any that ever existed is obsessed with the need to control events, nature, people, everything, should feel more than any other that things are out of control. But it is not a paradox; like a drowning man we clutch frantically at any fragments of certainty we can make or reach. We worship change and progress, the belief that the new must always be better than the old. We believe that we can change and improve on anything. And yet, we do not really believe that in any large sense we can change things to make them come out the way we like.

Thus the *Saturday Review of Science* recently published an article about what it called "the unspoiled places of the world." Note the implication that most of the world has already been spoiled. These unspoiled places are almost always remote islands, like the Seychelles in the Indian Ocean, and the writer said that more and more people, most of them rich, are flocking to these places from all over the world, to see them *before they are spoiled*. What an extraordinary statement about modern man. In one sense he believes that his powers are godlike. He can make any kind of machine, create energy from matter, travel all over the universe. But on a world in which he feels he has spoiled almost everything, he cannot imagine that he might be able to keep from spoiling the few places he has not yet spoiled. For that matter, how many people believe any more that the place they live in *right now,* be it city, town, neighborhood, or country, will in ten years be a better place? People hardly dream any more that this may be so, or that there is anything they might be able to do to make it so. The most they dare hope for is that they will be able to hold off disaster for a while and when disaster comes, will be rich enough to escape to some new unspoiled or less spoiled place and live in it for a while, until it too is spoiled.

We have created a false dream and called it Progress. Now that we see the dream is not coming true we are in despair, because we cannot imagine anything else. If newer and newer and more and more do not seem any longer to add up to the Good Life, we conclude there cannot be such a thing as a good life, and there is nothing for us to do but keep running on our treadmill as long as we can.

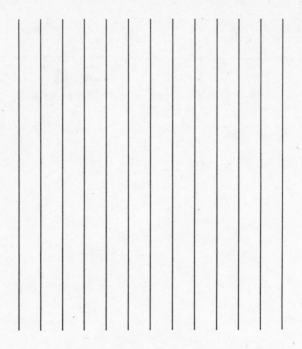

6. THE MANY "CRISES" OF LIFE

The gap we have made between childhood and the rest of life is only one of a number of growing gaps. The continuity of life is being broken at more and more places. We all know these days how much old people are cut off. For all our talk about "senior citizens" we all know that old age is a wasted and useless time of life. Nobody wants you, nobody is interested in you, you're a bother and a nuisance, you can't do anything, and you don't know anything, or what you know isn't worth knowing.

But this is by no means the only crisis or bad time in

life. A number of people, by all outward signs successful and happy, have told me that their fortieth birthdays came as a terrible shock to them. It seemed a sign that the best part of their lives was over. Indeed, we are more and more coming to think of human life as a series of crises—the crisis of puberty, the crisis of adolescence, the crisis of middle age, the crisis of old age. It is almost as if the only age to be is between twenty-one and thirty-five.

Only a few days after writing the above, I was going through Chicago, and in the *Chicago Tribune* of March 6, 1973, I read a story, entitled "Weathering the Storm of the Middle Years," by Ridgely Hunt, about a forthcoming conference of the American Medical Association. Hunt said (the *Tribune* has denied permission to quote directly) that in simpler times adults in their middle years didn't have time to worry about pollution, the quality of community schools, and so on, but that with the coming of leisure time many of them have now become frustrated over jobs, relations with their children, or their sex lives. He went on to say that in the following three days the AMA would examine the quality of life in the middle years, to see if they could find out what makes life so miserable for so many people and what might be done about it.

Three comments. I doubt very much that "in simpler times" anyone used or thought of such phrases as "the middle years." Nor did people worry much about anything as abstract and vague as "the quality of life." When they had problems, they knew what they were. Fire or insects or drought had destroyed their crops; plague was making them sick; their rulers were taxing them to death; war was killing them and laying waste to their land. And they knew what

61

had to be done about such problems, though they may not have been able to do it.

Finally, how typical it is of our times that we should think that this problem, that we are not living our lives well, or do not know how to live them, should be something that a group of "experts" can fix. This delusion, this modern superstition, lies very close to the heart of all our problems.

Hunt went on to say that Dr. Effie Ellis, an AMA official who helped plan the congress, considers the middle years "uncharted territory." I have to ask, uncharted by whom? Does the doctor mean that no one who lives through those middle years knows anything about them until some expert tells him what it all means?

Dr. Ellis described people so crushed by their jobs that they could not sleep at night, and went on to say that in earlier times the mere "struggle for survival" took so much of man's energy that he had no time for other problems, but that now he "enjoys the leisure" to fret over divorce, pollution, racism, growing old, unruly children, loss of his sexual powers, and so on. These worries make him fat and crabby, give him ulcers, high blood pressure, and heart disease, and cry out for relief.

But why does Dr. Ellis use the words "enjoy the leisure" to describe such a life? Why do most of us accept such words? They imply that the life that modern institutions have provided for us is a good one, only we are too stupid or mixed up to enjoy it so a group of experts has to get together to tell us how.

By the same token, it seems to me very unlikely that most of the human beings who have ever lived, doing the work they needed to do to get their food, clothing, and shelter and to maintain the structures of their community life, thought of this work as being a "struggle for survival." Is a person "struggling" when he raises food which he will eat, or makes clothing, or builds or fixes his dwelling? The notion is absurd. Only in times of crisis, when the food or fuel ran short, or war or disaster wiped out their homes, did people perhaps think of struggle. The trouble with modern man seems to me that he has made himself dependent on institutions that he can neither know or control. More and more he is not able, or even permitted, to act to meet his own basic needs. He can't even keep himself from getting "obese"—*i.e.,* fat—without a committee of experts telling him how to do it.

Such thoughts may seem a long way from concerns about children, but they are not. Later, when I talk about the right of a child to find his own protectors or to protect himself, I will refer back to this chapter. How can we tell children how to live their lives when we so clearly do not know how to live our own? Why should we expect them to pay any attention to us when we do tell them?

Hunt goes on to say that Dr. James Price, president-elect of the AMA, has said of his patients that 20 percent—infants in for "a well-child conference," adults in for a routine check or a physical exam—only want to improve or maintain a basically happy condition. Forty percent have specific organic ailments, about which the doctor can probably do something. The remaining 40 percent are what might be called victims of the quality of life. Half of these have diseases—ulcers, asthma, skin troubles—brought on by their worries; the other half have no identifiable disease at all, though their pain is real enough.

More comment. First, what is a "well-child conference"? Bad enough that when we *don't* feel well we think there is nothing to do but go to a doctor. Do we also have to go when

barbed wire into the garden. "They'd better learn," they say furiously, "what the world out there is really like."

For many years now, in all kinds of places and circumstances, I have noticed that most adults around children do not act as people do when they are with people they like, but very much the opposite. They are anxious, irritable, impatient, looking for fault and usually finding it. There is no ease, let alone joy. And this is true of people on vacation, or celebrating, or going to the park, or coming out of one of the big shows, or doing things that one might have supposed and hoped might be fun. There is always this air of strain, tension, conflict, and a frightening kind of patience that is not a good-humored acceptance but anger barely held back by an effort of will. Children alone in public places, unless cute —*i.e.,* very small, pretty, and dressed-up little girls—draw many hostile looks, as if to say, "What are you doing here? What are you up to? Where are your parents? Why aren't you with them? Why isn't some adult looking after you—*i.e.,* telling you what to do)?"

There are many good reasons for this resentment and dislike. Until recently, children were much less trouble to bring up. In a simpler society, if they survived their first years of life, they were soon useful. They earned their keep, and more. A man with many children was felt to be lucky. They were valuable property, a built-in labor force. Even where they could not be useful, or where their work was not needed, they didn't require so much watching. Towns and cities were less crowded, less dangerous, less car-ridden, and safer than they are now. There was more space for children to roam and play in. As recently as the late 1920s, when I first lived in Manhattan, the kind of daily traffic jam we now take for granted was rare, something we saw only in the heart of mid-town during holiday seasons. Major crosstown streets like 86th Street had little traffic on them, and many streets had few, if any, cars at all. A good friend of mine told me that some years later, growing up in Brooklyn, he and his friends used to play all day on the streets—football, stickball, hockey, and so on. Their mothers turned them out to play without having to watch or worry. When my family moved out of the city into the suburbs of Connecticut, my friends and I walked to many of the places that children now have to be driven to. We were by no means country children; we went to school in a bus, but if the weather was not bad we thought little of walking a mile or two to see a friend or go to a movie. The roads were safer; no one worried.

Perhaps when so many children died young of child-hood diseases, parents worried less about their being hurt or killed in other ways, or if they were, blamed themselves less for it. Perhaps they were simply too busy to worry. But bringing up children now is for many people an endless worry. One mother of a large family told me that from the birth of her first child until her last child became old enough to stop worrying about, she hardly ever had a decent night's sleep and was always tired. A mother of one baby can nap with the baby, but there seems to be some rule of nature that two small children hardly ever nap at the same time. Other women have spoken to me about this exhaustion.

The British novelist Margaret Drabble, in an article in the August 4, 1973, *New York Times* entitled "With All My Love, (Signed) Mama," a piece written in *defense and praise of having children,* had this to say:

Small children—toddlers, as they are rather offensively labled —are well known to be extremely exhausting. . . . I think

67

now that the pleasures of that stage are outweighed by the pains, though naturally I didn't think so at the time; but looking back, I wonder how I endured it. One is programmed to endure the most terrible things. And at this stage I must admit that an addiction to children is accompanied by the most frightful and serious disadvantages. It is all very well to recall the good moments, but what about all the bad times, the exhaustion, the illnesses, the bad temper and, worst of all, the endless, sickening anxiety? On the most profound level, once one has had children one can never be carefree again; each pleasure is snatched from the grave. They are hostages to fortune. I used to be a reasonably care-less and adventurous person, before I had children; now I am morbidly obsessed by seat belts and constantly afraid that low-flying aircraft will drop on my children's school.

The woman speaking here is not poor; she does the work she likes best; and she is competent, admired, and suc-cessful in this work. If this is how she feels about having children, how must all those women feel who are pressed by poverty or at least by worries about money and who, in fac-tory, shop, or home, do drudge work for little money or none at all? Not long ago, another parent wrote me:

It is a terrible emotional burden to have a child so com-pletely dependent on you—no safe place for him to play, no extended family for him to spend time with, etc. The result is that many mothers are *constantly* with their children— which is no better for the child than for the mother. For three years I was never away from K (she slept of course, but stopped taking naps at the age of 14 or 15 months) for more than two or three hours—and that was perhaps four times a year. This made me totally dependent on my husband for some sort of adult conversation, which was a burden on him. I was bored out of my mind and very short-tempered with K—I can understand how parents can beat their children. I came very close to it on two occasions—I know that if I had walked into her room or touched her I might well have done her serious damage. I was also exhausted, partly because I was bored—thinking on a two-year-old level can be very tiring when you do it twelve hours a day—and also because she only saw me and couldn't play outside. She was a mass of energy, which was always being bounced off me. It was all a bad scene—as a matter of fact, my idea of hell would be to be stuck with a small child or two in an apartment all alone again.

Above all, children are now an enormous expense. Not long ago the *Boston Globe* published a story saying that to raise a child these days, "from birth to B.A.," costs about $40,000. For people who want private schools, and many do, or for people whose children are sickly or get into accidents the figure is much higher. But it is a heavy burden on all, and even the poorest do not escape it. In many cities and towns, including one I know well, where about half the people are poor and many very poor, about a month before schools open in the fall, every clothing and department store in town begins to blossom with Back-To-School signs. The stores themselves, the papers, the radio, TV—all say Buy, Buy, Buy! Notebooks, supplies, lunch boxes, sports equipment, and, above all, clothes. Poor people flock into the stores and spend money they can't afford for all this stuff. They know that only rich children can afford to go to school in old or shabby or rough or informal clothes. Rich children almost always live in a rich neighborhood and go to a school where all the children are rich like themselves. Since the school knows they are rich, they can wear any clothes they want. But in schools where most of the children are poor, a child's standing and chances in school, the way teachers feel about him, the kind of track he gets put into, depend very much on how he looks. The more middle class he looks, the better the chance that the teacher will like him, help him, put him in a good track or reading section, and overlook or forgive his mistakes. So the poor dare not resist this appeal every year to send their children back to school in new clothes.

Modern childhood is an extraordinary emotional and financial burden. And as this burden has become heavier beyond anyone's wildest imagining, parents have been told ever more insistently that they have a *duty* to love their children, and the children that they have a duty to love their parents. We lock the old and young into this extraordinarily tense and troublesome relationship, and then tell them that they have to like it, even love it, and that if they don't they are bad or wrong or sick. There is no legitimate way for parents, staggering under this burden, to admit without shame or guilt that they don't much like these young people who live in their house, worry them half to death, and soak up most of their money, or that they wish they had never decided to have them in the first place, or that they could have had something different. The children on their part are expected to be grateful for what they did not ask for and often do not want.

Furthermore, when formerly a child became more help and less trouble as he grew older, today he becomes less help and more trouble. Everything he needs, uses, and wants costs more as he gets older—clothes, amusement, transportation, and, above all, schooling. And there are more kinds of trouble for him to get into, and what is worse, *to get his parents into*. How often we read about the parents of some young person who has committed some crime saying to reporters,

"We tried our best to bring him up right, keep him out of trouble, set a good example; we don't know what went wrong."

What makes the burden of having and raising children heaviest of all is an attitude or belief, perfectly expressed and cynically exploited in a commercial advertisement in the *New York Times* of Sunday September 9, 1973. At the top is a photo of a child—as we might expect, a girl, small, blond, pretty, looking solemn and thoughtful, a sentimental stereotype. The ad is headed:

EVERY NORMAL CHILD PRESENTS MATERIAL FOR
A MASTERPIECE OR A FAILURE

The ad then says, in part:

From birth most young children are "naturally" equipped to live deeply satisfying lives . . . but many will grow to be unhappy and frustrated. The future of every child is in the hands of his or her parent. You hold the brush! Masterpiece or failure?

You start out with good material, a healthy baby, pliable stuff. . . .

With all their unquestioned love and all their good intentions, mothers and fathers often lack the most efficient skills for this most important job in the world . . . building productive young lives through well-managed family living and skilled parenthood. . . .

Your family environment will create in your child a masterpiece or a forgery. . . .

This feeling that other people are judging you by what your child does or what you let him do is very strong. Here is a scene I have observed often. A mother is in some public place with a child, perhaps in a supermarket. She is busy and occupied; the child is moving happily and freely about, doing no harm, but looking at things, touching things, enjoying himself. Suddenly the mother notices another adult looking at her and the child. Instantly she puts on a show of authority, says to the child, "Come *here,* stop running around, how many times have I told you not to touch these things." Perhaps she gives him a sharp yank by the arm. This happens all the time, and in other countries as well. Lelia Berg, in her splendid and touching book *Look At Kids,* says that on buses or in public places in London, most adults, seeing children enjoying themselves, doing nothing harmful or wrong, will often look at them with expressions of disgust and rage and even voice their anger and contempt. The people in Britain who build adventure or construction playgrounds for children strongly recommended that they be closed in by a barrier through which and over which no one can see, not just to give children inside a feeling of privacy and ownership, but because the sight of children enjoying themselves arouses such rage in so many adults that the very existence of the playground may be threatened.

Nowhere is this fear, contempt, and even hatred more strongly expressed than in our schools. As by now many people know, Dr. Charles Silberman, for many years an editor of *Fortune* magazine, was commissioned by the Carnegie Foundation to do an extensive study of public schools in the U.S. What he and many other investigators found is in the book *Crisis In The Classroom,* in which in one place he writes:

It is not possible to spend any prolonged period visiting public school classrooms without being appalled by the mutilation visible everywhere—mutilation of spontaneity, of joy in learning, or pleasure in creating, or sense of self. . . . Because adults take the schools so much for granted, they fail to appreciate what grim, joyless places most American schools are [they are much the same in most countries], how oppressive and petty are the rules by which they are governed, how intellectually sterile and esthetically barren the atmosphere, what an appalling lack of civility obtains on the part of teachers and principals, what contempt they unconsciously display for students as students.

Strong words. And, we might note, Charles Silberman is no political radical, nor "a romantic," nor a sentimentalizer of children. What he saw, everyone who studies our schools in any depth sees. He thought that schools might be on the verge of getting better. Indeed, some are better. We read in the press many stories about schools where changes—many of them humane and interesting—are being made. On the other hand, some schools are worse. We hardly ever read about the schools, like the one described by Daniel Fader in *The Naked Children,* that made good changes and later gave them up. Most schools have changed very little. The textbooks and gadgetry have been updated, a lot of new buildings have been built, but the spirit, on the whole, is what it always was. The reason is that this is what the public wants. Indeed, every poll that I have seen shows that a majority want the schools to be even more rigid, threatening, and punitive than they are, and they will probably become so.

The walled garden, then, turns out much of the time, for many people in it, to be not better than the big world outside, but worse—even more competitive, contemptuous, and cruel.

"They have to find out, don't they, what reality is all

about, what that world out there is like? Well, the sooner they learn, the better." So say the keepers of the garden. But if our concern is to teach them, not protect them from, the bad ways of the world, why not let them out into it where they can see and learn for themselves?

8. ONE USE OF CHILDHOOD

Children, and the institution of childhood, though a great burden and nuisance, do have some important uses. Children may not be able any more to do much of the work of the family or add to its income. But at least for a while, they do give the adults in the family something that most adults need very much—someone to boss, someone to "help," someone to love.

For a very long time, ever since men formed societies in which some people bossed others, children have fulfilled this very important function. Every adult parent, however lowly or powerless, had at least someone that he could command, threaten, and punish. No man was so poor, even a slave, that he could not have these few slaves of his own. Today, when most "free" men feel like slaves, having their own home-grown slaves is very satisfying. Many could not do without them.

The other day in the subway I saw a mini-drama that over the years I have seen enacted many times. A man came into the car with his son, about eight years old. There were plenty of seats, but the man preferred to stand. However, he wanted the boy to sit. Without looking at him, or even look-ing in his direction, his face and voice utterly without expres-sion, he said in a barely audible monotone, "Sit!" He accom-panied this command with a brief downward gesture of his hand, the kind of gesture one might make to a dog—except that I have heard very few people talk to their dogs as this man talked to his son. The boy sat down immediately—no one could have missed the threat of anger and violence in his father's voice and gesture.

Most children, some time during their growing up, be-come aware that much of the time their parents talk to them as they do not talk and would not dare to talk to any other people in the world. Of course, we justify ourselves in doing this, as in all our exercise of power over the young, by saying that we have their best interests at heart, are only doing it because we love them—like the proverbial parent saying be-fore the spanking, "This hurts me more than it does you."—perhaps one of the world's oldest lies.

A friend tells me that on some TV comedy show she saw a skit taking off the way so many parents treat their children but would never treat other adults. In the skit some people had invited another couple over to dinner, and said to the guests such things as: "Get off my chair, will you. I work hard all day and can't even have my own favorite chair when I come home." And, "How many times do I have to tell you to wash your damned hands before you eat?"—and much similar swearing and shouting at the astonished guests.

And so the family home, which we often hear described as the place where we are free to be and dare to be nicer and kinder than we can be anywhere else, turns out much of the time to be the place where at least to our children we can be harsher, more cruel, more contemptuous and insulting, than we would be anywhere else. This supposed refuge for the young becomes the place of greatest danger, where they can get in more and worse trouble than anywhere else, and with people whose support and protection they most depend on.

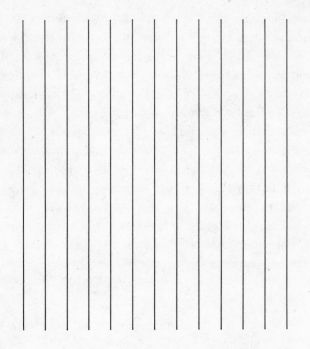

9. ON "HELP" AND "HELPERS"

About a year or so ago someone told me a great truth about helpers and help—The Helping Hand Strikes Again!

Many people laugh in surprise when they first hear this. Then they draw back and say, hold on now, wait a minute. For in its best sense, there is nothing wrong at all with the idea of helping those who need help. The Good Samaritan who helped the injured traveler in the ditch is one of our culture heroes for good reasons. We need more like him. But when the traveler was healed and well, the Good Samaritan let him go on his way. He did not tell him he could not travel because it was so dangerous or because obviously he couldn't take care of himself. He did not make himself a permanent protector of the traveler. He did not make a business or career or vocation out of protecting all travelers. He helped because, before his eyes, he could see someone who at that moment needed help. Otherwise he had other things to do.

It is important that we try to understand how the idea of help has been so largely corrupted and turned into a destructive exploitation, how the human act of helping is turned more and more into a commodity, an industry, and a monopoly. I am troubled by anyone who wants to make a lifework out of being, usually without being asked, the helper and protector of someone else. The trouble with one person defining himself as a helper of others is that unless he is very careful he is almost certain to define them as *people who cannot get along without his help*. He may say this to them, or try hard to persuade them of it; he may say nothing, and keep the thought to himself; or he may not even be aware of the thought. In all cases the result is likely to be the same. His way of dealing with those he is helping, what he does and what he says (or refuses to say) about what he does, are almost sure to convince them that they do in fact depend on his help.

The person whose main lifework is helping others needs and must have others who need his help. The helper feeds and thrives on helplessness, creates the helplessness he needs. The trouble with the helping professions—teaching, psychiatry, psychology, social work—is that they tend to attract people who want to play God. Some of them, perhaps most of them, want to play a kindly and benevolent God; others,

79

and perhaps without knowing it, may want to play a harsh and cruel God, to take out of the hides of others what some earlier God took out of theirs. In either case the effect is much the same. For a person can only play God if he can make other people into his puppets. And, as the early Christians knew, it does not take much frustration to turn a God into a Devil.

Over and over again, we see this cycle repeated. The helper begins by saying to someone, "Let me do that for you, I know more about it, I can do it better than you." Soon he says, "Don't do that, you are not able to do it for yourself." Soon after that he says, "I will not allow you even to try to do that for yourself, you will make a mistake, hurt yourself or someone else." For the other to reject his help begins as ingratitude or a foolish mistake; it soon becomes a sin and a crime.

No one is more truly helpless, more completely a victim, than he who can neither choose nor change nor escape his protectors. Here, for example, is a description of what life is like in one of these "protecting" institutions, a "home" for retarded children run by the State of New York. An article, "Another Unhappy Year at Willowbrook," by Robin Reisic, in the *Village Voice* (New York City) of December 28, 1972, said, in part:

> A year ago on Christmas David (a retarded child at the institution) was burned on his face, ear, chest, and wrist. This Christmas he could look back on a year in which he had a fractured nose (which wasn't x-rayed until two days after the fracture), a fractured finger, and gashes requiring stitches on his head at least six times. When he was 10 years old, David, who is mentally retarded, was toilet-trained, ate

politely, and talked happily with his parents. Now, after two years at Willowbrook, he "soils his bed," said his mother, "I can't describe how he eats, I hate to sit next to him," and "he carries on conversations only with himself."

Last week . . . before Federal District Judge Orrin Judd . . . one father told how he saw his son Stevie's face was swollen and his eye was closed when he visited him one week. He asked for his son to see a doctor, asked again the next week, and finally wrote and pleaded that his son be examined. Finally a doctor examined Stevie, and operated, and told his father "It's too late"—Stevie had lost an eye.

One mother showed photo after photo of her daughter with gashes on her head, cuts, scratches, black eyes, bloated lips. Another mother told how her daughter was placed in seclusion (solitary confinement—a practice against the rules of the commission accrediting institutions). Week after week she lay in just a pajama top "on a stone cold floor"—until she caught pneumonia.

Some photos of the residents' injuries showed bruises that were clearly shaped like keys, and Bill Bronston, a Willowbrook staff physician, testified to finding the key-shaped marks on residents. Residents do not carry keys. Only the staff carries keys. . . .

In defense, the state says that the federal courts have no jurisdiction, that conditions at Willowbrook cannot be defined as "cruel and unusual punishment" for residents who were *voluntarily committed*. (Italics mine—J.H.)

The article raised questions it did not answer. There do exist private institutions for retarded children in which children are not mistreated but well treated. People I know have children in them. But these cost a lot of money. Presumably Willowbrook, like other state-run and tax-supported institutions, is for the children of the people who don't have that much money. One wonders why such people, finding their children so brutally mistreated, don't take them out. The answer probably varies from family to family. In many cases, the children need a special kind of care which the parents themselves, perhaps because they are both working, cannot give. Or perhaps they have to send their "retarded" children to Willowbrook because the other institution that the state provides to get children out of the way of adults, the school, will not take them. Or perhaps they have been convinced by some expert that institutional care is the best thing for their child. Or perhaps the shame and strain of having a retarded child in the house is more than they can bear, or choose to bear. In any case, it is most likely that they put their child in a state institution only after much painful soul-searching and that they feel they have no choice but to keep him there and to try to do what little they can to get the state to treat him decently. Since the state runs on votes, and since there are not many votes in the issue of better institutional care (which costs money), they don't have much choice.

But we don't have to look only at retarded children to see what can and does happen to people who cannot choose or escape their protectors. Not long ago I read a story written by a woman whose mother had recently died of some prolonged and incurable (but endlessly treatable) illness, in a hospital in which *she was paying for her care*. The sick and dying woman quite naturally lost her appetite and ate hardly any of the food that the hospital gave her. They told her that she *had* to eat though they knew she could not get well and would never leave the hospital alive. When she continued to refuse, they began to force-feed her through a tube in her nose, which (for their convenience) they apparently left in all the time. This was not only an indignity but uncomfortable, so the sick woman took out this tube whenever she could. This made extra work for the nurses, who had to put the tube back each time to feed this woman who had no further interest in prolonging her life—if we can call such existence "life." So they solved their problem by the simple expedient of *tying the woman's hands to the bed*. All the time! She spent most of her conscious hours during the last months of her life *pleading* with anyone who might hear her to untie her hands. We can only pray to be spared such helpers and protectors.

Some say that such criticism is not true of helping institutions as such but only of certain American institutions, that in some other countries helpless people are not so callously and cruelly treated and helping institutions truly help rather than hurt the people in them. Perhaps so. From reports, some countries in Europe seem to have a stronger sense of social compassion and social justice than we do. Perhaps it is because they are smaller, more homogenous, and older countries. Perhaps their great suffering under the Nazis in World War II, which everybody shared, pulled them together and gave them a strong sense of common identity and concern, made them feel like a large family (in the best sense). But such a feeling is at best fragile, easily worn away by time, greed, and social pressures.

The nightmare state of the future, if it comes, and it is well on its way, will be above all a tyranny of "professional helpers," with an unlimited right and power to do to us or

83

make us do whatever they (or someone) considers to be for our own good. It should not surprise us that the Russian police state now puts in "mental hospitals" those who strongly and publicly object to its way of doing things and there subjects them to "treatment" until they think or act as they are supposed to. Or that the miniature police states of our schools are more and more using strong drugs such as Ritalin on those children who do not, or will not, fit smoothly into its regime. How far is it from the compulsory dosage of psychoactive and dangerous drugs—and let us be clear about it, it *is* compulsory and the drugs *are* dangerous —to the planting of miniature electrodes in the brain, perhaps tuned to a transmitter on the teacher's desk or in her hand, so that she can instantly zap little Willie with some positive or negative reinforcement (*i.e.,* pain) as the occasion seems to demand. Scientists are working on these things.

Of all people in history who have coerced, threatened, and hurt other people there have been very few honest enough to see and candid enough to say, "I am doing this to you, or forcing you to do this for me, not for your good but *mine*." Most of them claim, usually sincerely, to act from the highest motives. Even the Inquisitors pulling people apart on the rack believed they were trying to save their screaming victims from eternal hell-fire. Clearly this justified whatever present suffering they might be causing them. Wherever torturers have been at work, they have almost always been working in the name of some higher good.

We can not assume, just because we hear someone say, "I am doing this to help you," that what he does will be good. It may very well be bad. The good intention does not *of itself* excuse or justify the act. The helping act must be judged by and for itself. The burden of proof must always be on the helper to show that he is in fact helping.

Even this is not enough. There is no way to be *sure* that compulsory helpers will be kind, competent, and unselfish, or that their help will be really helpful and will not turn into exploitation, domination, and tyranny. The only remedy is to give to everyone the right to decide if, and when, and by whom, and for how long, and in what way, he will choose to be helped.

Not all helpers are would-be tyrants—this is part of what makes them dangerous. They are often just people who worry about other people making mistakes. They talk as if they thought that with enough expert knowledge men really could find ways to prevent other people from ever making any mistakes. They assume that if we have such power, of course we have the right and even a duty to use it. In meetings they sometimes accuse me of thinking that without "help" nobody would make any mistakes, or of not caring whether they make them or not. Neither is true. Most people in the course of their lives will make plenty of mistakes. I insist on their right to do so. What I believe is that given any real choices and alternatives almost everyone will manage his life better than anyone else, however expert, could manage it for him and that if and when he does make mistakes, if he is not locked into them, he will be quicker than anyone else to recognize and change them.

What we need to realize, and it is often very hard in the case of people we love, is that our power over another person's life is at most very limited and that if we try to extend our power beyond that narrow limit we do so only by taking from him his ability to control his own life. The only way we can fully protect someone against his own mistakes and the uncertainties of the world is to make him a slave. He is then defenseless before *our* whims and weaknesses. Most people would prefer to take their chances with the world. They have the right to that choice.

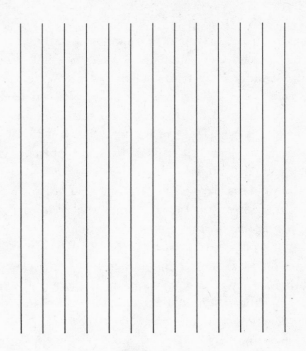

10. THE COMPETENCE OF CHILDREN

Returning to Boston not long ago I was walking through the air terminal when I spied ahead of me a mother and child walking in the same direction. The child was dressed in a bright yellow puffed-out snowsuit. From his size, and the way he walked, he seemed at most a year and a half or two years old. His mother was holding his hand, and I could see that as he walked he was stubbornly but futilely trying to get it free. He kept pulling it and twisting his arm and shoulder away from her grip. Clearly he wanted to take this walk by himself.

His mother may have been holding his hand from nothing more than habit. I wondered, suppose I could put in her mind the thought, "Why don't I let go of his hand, which he obviously wants, and let him walk by himself?" She might then have thought, "Why not?" and tried it. But from the firmness of her grip it seemed more likely that she would think or say, "I can't let go of his hand, he's not yet two, if I let go he'll run off, get knocked down by someone, get in trouble, get hurt, do some mad and foolish and dangerous thing. I just don't dare take the chance." This was possible but not likely. Probably the child only wanted to walk along beside his mother in that stream of people, just like everyone else. It would have been easy to let him try. If the child had started to walk away, the mother could have caught up with him in a step or two. A small thing, no doubt. But there was an opportunity missed, to give that child a chance to feel independent and trusted, to be like other people, and do what they were doing.

At another time, in another airport, I saw a parent, this time a father, with a child no older, waiting for a plane. The child wanted to walk around and explore, and the father was wise and kind enough to let him. As the child walked about in the waiting area and corridor, the man followed him, not so close as to make the child feel that he was being followed or pursued (which usually makes little children *want* to run) but close enough so that if the child got near anything that might hurt him, the father could move in and prevent it. Also, he stayed just close enough so that now and then, when the child in the middle of his exploring would suddenly think, "Where is Daddy?" and would look around for a glimpse of a familiar face, he could find it. It was a wonderfully tactful and sensitive kind of supervision. The child wandered happily about, over not too great an area—for most small children are timid as well as bold—until he grew tired of exploring altogether and wanted a rest.

At the baggage claim I saw a similar scene. Here was a young mother with two children, a boy of about six or seven, a girl of about four or five. The conveyor belt had already begun to move, though there were no bags on it, and this was fascinating to the children. They came close to look at it and also to see the hole in the wall through which the bags would appear. From their curiosity and eagerness I would guess that they had never before seen anything quite like this. But no sooner had they started to look than their mother, in an irritable voice, began to say, "Keep away from that, don't touch it." They had made no move to touch it; they only wanted to look at it and to see the bags coming in. Without standing as close as the people waiting for the luggage, they could not see at all. Their curiosity being strong, they kept pressing forward, peering around the bigger people to look at the exciting mystery. From time to time the mother, in the same vexed voice, would order them to get back, not to touch (which they were still not doing), to stand by her (where they could see nothing). This quiet struggle went on until my bag arrived and I left.

I don't tell this story to blame the mother. Many anxieties may have been pressing on her. For all I know the children may have earlier made terrible nuisances of themselves or almost got themselves into some sort of trouble or danger. The point is, what does this kind of adult anxiety do to children, what does it tell them about themselves and about the world around them and their ability to cope with it? Clearly it tells them: (1) the world is a terribly dangerous, treacherous, unpredictable place; (2) you are wholly unable to cope with it and must depend on me to keep you out of all kinds of trouble.

Perhaps someday this anxious mother, now so determined to curb her children's curiosity, will be worried about their reading, their schooling, their education, about "how to motivate them," about "how to get them to learn." Perhaps someday she will join the many adults who say sadly, "My child doesn't seem to be interested in anything." By then it may well be true, though her children may simply have learned that if they are interested in something it is better not to let Mom know about it. But how can we expect to spend years damping and denying children's curiosity, and teaching them to distrust and fear it as something that can only get them into trouble, and then later expect that they will be eager and adept learners?

Later, on one of my lecture trips, I met a very intelligent and competent woman, who had the task of driving me from meeting to meeting. At one point in our conversation she told me about her nine-year-old daughter, who had learned to cook and also learned to like many kinds of food that she would not eat until she started to cook them. The mother talked a bit about her daughter's skill in cooking. Then she said, "But every time she starts to cook I am afraid that she will burn herself or hurt something." I thought but did not say, "How long does your daughter have to cook without burning herself before you stop assuming she is going to do it? What does she have to do to earn your confidence?"

We underestimate so much and so continually both the competence and the drive for competence in the young. *Esquire* magazine, a few years ago, devoted an issue to what is called the "micro-boppers"—its own word for people younger than "teeny-boppers" (people in their mid-teens)—who were then much in the news. There were a number of articles about the supposed precocity of young people under twelve. One told of a radio station run almost entirely by people under twelve. The station was connected with a local school, and the rule was that whenever someone working in the station passed the age of twelve he had to move out to make room for someone younger. According to the article, they prepared and broadcast a wide range of program materials, and at a high level of competence.

Young people have to be trained, in part by what we tell them, mostly by how we treat them, to think of themselves as irresponsible, incompetent, ignorant, foolish, no-account. This is an important part of what childhood is all about, what it does, what it is for. In a society which people did not assume such things of the young they would not assume it of themselves.

I was once interviewed by radio station WBAI in New York City. I talked about the institution of childhood and of the great potentialities and capacities of young people, which we do not use or even acknowledge. Many calls came in during the program, more than we could answer in the time we had. As I was leaving the studio, a man who had been trying to call finally got through. The WBAI people said that he very much wanted to talk to me and asked if I would talk to him, which I did. He told me a most interesting story. He was a dental technician, head of a laboratory associated with a large dental clinic somewhere near New York City. Over the years, he had trained the front office to tell him whenever a young person of about ten or eleven came in with a parent who was going to have extensive work done. When they told him this, he would go to the office, spot the young person and say, "Since you are going to be here for a few hours while your mother/father is getting the work done, would you like to come out and see the lab?" In almost every case the young person would say yes. Off they would go; he would take a tour of the lab and show all the kinds of work they were doing. If the young person seemed interested, as he almost always was, he would then ask, "How would you like to help me out with some work I am doing?" Again, the young person would almost always say yes. And he would put him to work. The point was that there was almost always some real work that the young person could do. Telling me this, the lab head said, "I wish I could hire lab help as bright, curious, eager and quick to learn, and energetic as those ten-year-old kids. By the time they do come to me, when the law finally allows them to work, they have had most of the energy, curiosity, confidence, and willingness knocked out of them."

A ninth grade student worked a week in my office with two of my colleagues who were trying to persuade various branches of the city government to let them organize an adventure or construction playground in one part of the city. The student wrote letters, made phone calls, visited various city offices, did errands, talked to people, did real work, and was very useful. At the end of the week, when she had to go back to regular school work, she said wistfully how much she had loved working and wished she could go on. It is true that the work she was doing was more varied and interesting than what most people do. The point is that she did it very well.

J. H. van den Berg tells of a sixteen-year-old who, in time of war, was sent somewhere in Holland to take charge of a garrison. I recall reading when I studied naval history in the NROTC that during our Revolutionary War fourteen-year-olds were often midshipmen—the lowest-ranked naval officer—and at least one sixteen-year-old was in command of his own ship, a far more difficult and responsible task than most people ever do in a lifetime. The anthropologist Edward Hall, now living in the Southwest and very much interested in its history, told me of reading the records of a large wagon train that a century or so ago had come from the middle of the U.S. to New Mexico under the command of a young man of fourteen. And Paul Murray Kendall writes in *Richard III* (W.W. Norton Co., 1955): "(King) Edward scraped together every penny he could lay hands on, and he dispatched commissions of array for twenty-two countries, the whole southern half of England. . . . Customarily a half-dozen or more men were appointed commissioners for each county. . . . In this case, however, Richard, Duke of Gloucester, was made sole commissioner for nine of the twenty-two counties. . . . It appears that Richard, in his twelfth year, had been entrusted by his royal brother with the surprising responsible charge of levying troops from a quarter of the realm."

When we read about what we call the precocity of some children of earlier times, we are skeptical, often deeply threatened. The very words "precocity" and "precocious" sound like the names of diseases. They betray our feelings that most children could not possibly have done such things and that a child who could and did must have been something of a freak. Many are so used to a sentimental and condescending view of children that when they hear of a child of four speaking Latin and Greek they feel a kind of horror. Yet there is nothing remarkable about this, even now; children who have regular contact with people who speak several languages will learn all these languages as easily as most children learn one. During the year I went to school in Switzerland I knew a number of boys twelve years old or younger, from small European countries, who spoke three or four languages. No one thought it surprising; if you lived in a small country, and traveled much, that is what you did.

Perhaps it is in music that we are most used to hearing of child prodigies. Even there we don't like it, and we assume that something must be wrong with the child, that he has been pressured into becoming some kind of freak. But as the Japanese musician and teacher Suzuki has shown us: (1) children of six, five, or even four can learn to play the violin with an astonishing degree of proficiency; (2) large numbers of "average" children are able to do this, not just a few rare geniuses; (3) children can do this without devoting all their lives to the violin, without being damaged, stunted, or "robbed of their childhood." By now Suzuki-trained children have come to the United States a number of times and every time astonished people by the skill and musicality of their playing. These children, as Suzuki pointed out at the concert where I first heard them, have by no means been specially picked out as the most promising pupils—they are special only in that their parents can afford to pay for the trip and that their mothers can go with them. But there are thousands back in Japan who play as well as they do. Furthermore, by signs I have learned to trust, the children that I heard play a number of years ago in Boston were very healthy, happy, lively children, in no way afraid of Suzuki, obviously enjoying what they were doing, full of life, energy, and fun.

This is not a pitch for Suzuki violin training. He is important as a teacher because, as he himself said, he realized one day that if almost all Japanese children could learn to speak Japanese, a difficult task requiring very complicated coordination, then most of them were obviously capable of learning to play the violin. Why the violin? Partly because it was his instrument, partly because (unlike wind instruments) it can be scaled down to the size of the child, partly because even a very small child has the strength to play it, and partly because with a stringed instrument it is possible to move to a correct note, as to a correctly spoken sound, by successive small steps—you can *find* a note on a violin, as you cannot on a wind or brass instrument. In short, because if we come to them in a proper spirit, and with a proper understanding of the ways in which we learn things (which is not at all like the ways in which most people try to teach us things), the violin (and other stringed instruments) are not the hardest but the easiest instruments to learn to play.

By contrast, I think of a school, probably typical of many American pre-schools, in which four- and five-year-old children are formed into what is called a rhythm band. Using small drums, bells, and cymbals, they beat out, more or less, the rhythm of some piece that the teacher plays for them. The children, like the teacher, believe that what they are doing is very close to the limit of what they can do, and invite us to marvel at it. All the while children of no greater natural ability, in Japan, are playing on their real violins music by Vivaldi, Handel, and Bach.

After my visit to the Children's Community in Ann Arbor, in the days when it was thriving, when the time came to take me to the airport at Detroit, Bill Ayers asked how many of the children wanted to go with us. Five of them, none older than five, said they did. Off we went, three children in the back, one in the seat between Bill and myself, one in my lap. As we drove along we turned the radio to one of the local stations playing popular music—blues, rock, Motown. To my astonishment these very young children sang along word for word and note for note with this music, in rhythm and melody twenty times more subtle and complicated than anything they would hear in a conventional school.

Some years ago there was talk in the media about a then-prodigy, a boy of about eight named Joey Alfidi, who as I recall played the piano quite skillfully, had written some quite complicated music of his own, and had conducted a symphony orchestra—even made a recording (I think the symphony he conducted was Beethoven's Eighth). I don't know what if anything he has done with music since. Some such child prodigies maintain their interest in music and develop their talents; in our time, the conductor Lorin Maazel and the violinist Yehudi Menuhin are well-known examples. Others do not. Either way is okay by me. I suspect that such children who get very good at music do so not so much because people are forcing them to practice—millions of children are forced to practice who never get any good—but because they are surrounded by people who love music and make music and above all because no one around them thinks that it is impossible for young people to be musically skillful.

The words "expect" and "expectation" are on the whole badly misunderstood and misused by most people who write about children. Most people use them as synonyms for "demand" or "insist" or "compel." When they say we should have higher expectations of children, they mean that we should demand that they do certain things and threaten to punish them if they do not. When I speak of expecting a lot of children, I only mean that we should not in our minds put an upper limit on what they may be able to do. I don't mean we should assume that they can, and therefore should, do certain things or be disappointed and worried if they do not —everyone has his own path and timetable into life. I do mean that we should not assume that there are things that they cannot do or be astonished and even threatened when they do them. We should be open to their way of growing, whatever it may be. With this understanding of the word, I believe that if we expected more from children, and they from themselves, they would be able to learn much more about the world around them, much more quickly, than they do now. Or, to put it differently, they would go on exploring and learning after the age of three as eagerly and capably as they did in their first three years.

In my own life I am much more often a passenger in a car than a driver. Others drive me from one place to another. In this situation I pay little attention to where we are going but look at the surroundings much as a child does, with a kind of open unfocused interest. But if on the other hand I am driving to a place from which I will have to drive back, or to which I will later have to drive myself, I pay a closer attention, look at turning points, make a note of the surroundings, think about what a turn will look like coming back the other way, and so on.

If children do not learn the ropes faster in our society, and even now they learn them faster than we think, it is in part because they do not have to, are not expected to, and do not expect themselves to, and in part because they know that they could not do anything with the knowledge if they had it. Suppose, when we frequently took children to a place, we said to them that after a certain point we would let them be the guides. Suppose, walking 'round town with children, we pretended to be strangers and at each corner let them tell us which way to go. Would they not learn much more quickly how to find their way around their neighborhoods, towns, and cities, how to get information from the surroundings, how to ask questions of other people?

Not long ago I saw a striking, almost unbelievable, example of this in the main building of the Copenhagen airport, on the morning of Midsummer's Day. My plane was not leaving for a couple of hours, and I was standing around in the main waiting room, until the bank opened and I could change some money, and meanwhile looking at the crowds of people meeting friends or going places. One large group of people seemed to be waiting to go someplace together. They stood in a long line amidst their luggage, talking to each other. One of them had two children with her, the older about four years old, the younger between two and three. They were very excited, curious, and active, and I entertained myself watching them. They ran around in and amongst the people standing in line and other groups coming in or out of the airport. The younger child was the more adventurous of the two. Often he was quite out of sight of his mother, but it did not seem to trouble him. The two of them, after chasing each other or running around for a while, would make their way back to their mother, perhaps exchange a few words, and then go off again. The mother, talking with friends, seemed wholly unconcerned, or wholly confident. She was busy talking and did not appear to be keeping an eye on her children at all. I admired her confidence, but could not keep from worrying from time to time whether the children might not have trouble, in all those crowds, finding their way back to her. But they always did, and when they looked for her, they did so without anxiety. They were as casual and systematic as I might have been looking for a ticket counter.

As time went on, they became more and more curious about the airport itself and the shops, newsstands, and restaurants in it. They began to explore, each time getting further from their mother, and each time finding their way back. Finally the little one took off at a run for the far end of the building, 200 or more feet away. The other one followed after, this time looking nervously now and then back in the direction of the mother. I too was a little nervous. I thought that when they came to the far end of the building, and turned around to see that huge space before them, with their mother nowhere in sight, they might panic. I walked unobtrusively toward the end of the room, a little over to the side, ready to show them the way back if they should need help. But there was no need; the little one, after exploring the end of the room, and pushing at a few doors, turned around and, again on the dead run, headed straight back for his mother, the relieved older one following. They stayed with her for only a few seconds before running off again. This time they began to investigate the automatic sliding doors at the entrance. For a while they watched the doors opening and closing as people came in and out. Then they made an experiment or two, and in no time had figured out how to work the doors themselves. They amused themselves doing this for a while. Then the younger one decided to investigate what was outside. A big bus had pulled up in front of the door, and he went out through the sliding doors to get a good look at it. I watched him through the doors, beginning to feel a little nervous again. For a while he was happy to watch the people getting off the bus. Suddenly he turned and went off down the sidewalk, out of sight. I thought, "This is really too much," and quickly went outside to keep an eye on him, though still without appearing to watch him. He had gone up the platform to look at some other buses. I wondered what would happen next. Had he forgotten his mother? Would he be drawn further and further away by one interesting sight after another? Or if he decided to go back to the waiting room and his mother, would he be able to find the way? Or would I, perhaps with the aid of someone who could speak Danish, have to show him the way? But again, there was no need to worry. When he had had enough of looking at buses he turned and without the slightest hesitation or confusion went to the entrance, through the doors, and back to his mother, who greeted him without surprise or alarm. Shortly thereafter their group began to move toward wherever they were going, and I saw no more of them.

This child was clearly able to do what we think of children as being wholly unable to do until they are much older. He was able to use what he could see of his surroundings to make a mental map that would enable him to find his way around, I can only guess that he had had much practice doing this, that his mother regularly allowed him to explore the territory around him. Perhaps at first she had followed him anxiously, as I did, but then gained confidence in him as he gained skill and confidence in himself and gave him a chance to explore larger and larger pieces of territory. I will never know by what means this so-young child came to have such skill. But what he could do, surely many others could do. If we gave up our vested interest in children's dependency and incompetence—would they not much more quickly become independent and competent? We ought to give it a try.

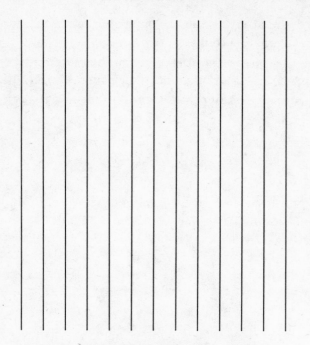

11. THE CHILD AS LOVE OBJECT

Years ago, a friend of mine used to tell a very funny Embarrassing Moment story. Hearing of a sale at one of New York's large department stores, she went there early, like many other women, to find some good bargains before they were all snapped up. As soon as the doors opened in she went, in a dense crowd of hurrying people. As she walked along, she found herself just behind two small boys whose heads came up only a little above her waist. Feeling affectionate and mischievous, she put a fingertip on the top of each boy's head and walked along that way for a step or two.

But no more than that; in an instant, two furious adult faces looked up at her and in a harsh, high, but adult voice one of them said, "What the hell do you think you're doing?" They were midgets!

Over the years I have heard her tell this story several times and every time joined others in laughing at it. Only after many years, really quite recently, did I realize that behind her act and our laughter was this thought—that if those midgets really had been children, it would have been perfectly all right to walk along with her fingertips on the tops of their heads. What made the story so funny was that what seemed to be such a good idea, the sort of thing that all of us child-lovers would like to do, turned out so quickly to be such a bad idea. We laughed because we could so easily put ourselves into her shoes, imagine ourselves with hearts brimming with love, putting our fingers on the dear little children's heads, and imagine our horror at finding our mistake. But what makes it such a good idea to walk along with our fingers on the tops of strange children's heads? What gives us the right to do it? What gives us the right to think that they like us to do it?

We treat someone as an object when we use him for our purposes, to achieve our ends, to get things for ourselves, without considering or caring what this does to him or how he feels about it, without asking what he gets out of it or whether he gets anything at all. Many women complain with good reason that most men use them, or would like to use them, as sex objects. Such men believe that if not in reality at least in fantasy they have a right to use all women for their sexual satisfaction. Many men, especially young men, habitually "size up" every woman they see. That is they think about what the woman would look like naked and what it might be

like to have sex with her. They make a quick judgement—
"Terrific lay!" "Okay." "Not so hot." "Ugh!" If the judgement is favorable, they spend a moment or two, or more,
having fantasy sex with her. Some may even try to turn their
fantasies into reality. If the judgement is bad, they dismiss
the woman from thought. They do not think of her in any
other way. She has no other interest for them.

A man uses a woman (or perhaps a woman a man) as a
sex object if in reality or in his mind, and without her consent, he uses her for his needs without considering hers. In
our culture men are encouraged to use women this way by
all they see—in advertising, the media, and the world around
them—that displays women as sex objects. Many women co-
operate in this and willingly display themselves so, for money
or "to get a man"—boy friend, lover, or husband. But the sex
object industry, the business of selling women as sex objects,
is largely run by men for the profit of men.

The habit of using women as sex objects may explain why
seeing other men with long hair used to make, or still makes,
some men so irrationally angry. Such longhairs, by their de-
ceiving appearance, may trick other men into fantasy sexual,
and therefore homosexual, relations with them. A taxi driver,
passing one such young man, once said furiously to me, "You
can't tell the boys from the girls!" I said, "Well, as long as
they can tell the difference it's probably okay." He said, "The
hell it's okay!" It did not seem a good time to ask him why
it was so important for him to be able to tell the difference.
Another driver in the same situation said in a voice choked
with rage, "They all oughta be shot!" Why was it so important for those men to be able to tell at a glance the boys from
the girls? One reason may be that only in this way could they
be sure with whom they might be free to have fantasy sex.

Otherwise they might be daydreaming about having a great time in bed with some girl, only to find out suddenly that "she" was a boy. It is almost as if the longhairs were trying to trick them into being homosexuals.

These ideas about women and men are well understood —at least, more people understand them all the time. They may make more clear what I mean in saying that almost all adults, men and women, use children as what we might call love objects. We think we have a right, or even a duty, to bestow on them "love," visible and tangible signs of affection, whenever we want, however we want, and whether they like it or not. In this we exploit them, use them for our purposes. This, more than anything else, is what we use children and childhood for—to provide us with love objects. This is why we adults find children worth owning and the institution of childhood worth preserving, in spite of their great trouble and expense.

One reason we need and use children for this purpose is that many of us are so starved for human contact and affection. Most people have only a few other people to whom they may legitimately give affection and fewer yet to whom they may openly express it with words of endearment or physical contact. In this respect women may be better off than men. Perhaps because they are sex objects themselves, or perhaps because society considers them an inferior class and therefore allowed certain licenses, they are permitted more than men to touch other people, both men and women. Men are really only supposed to touch the women to whom they are closely related, and they are not supposed to touch other men in any affectionate way at all.

We are not supposed to *love* our friends. Most men who said with warmth and conviction of another man, "I really love him," would be deeply suspect. Even women who say it may be considered over-emotional. We are not supposed to *love* any other than very close blood relatives—children, parents, grandparents, grandchildren. Even aunts, uncles, and cousins are not really included in this love-permitting circle.

For these reasons, anyone to whom we can give affection and love, openly and physically, any time and any place we feel like it, whenever the mood or need strikes us, without danger or shame, and indeed knowing we will gain general approval—such a person is immeasurably useful and valuable to us. We desperately need these love objects. It is very painful to have more love to give away than people to whom we can give it. This is what hurts so much about unrequited love—not only does the loved one not love us but also does not want our love and will not allow us to love him. We offer our finest treasures, but he does not want them. What then are we to do with them?

Many who have written about their childhood have described the frightening and disgusting feelings of being embraced or kissed by an adult they did not like and whose appearance and manner revolted them. To such talk a friend of mine once said that perhaps the older person *needed* to kiss the small child and so it was right to compel the child to let him do it. This is a perfect example of what I mean about an adult using a child. If the needs of a four-year-old and a sixty-year-old come into conflict, why must the child always give way? Is he entitled to no consideration simply because he is smaller and weaker? For that matter, any adult who is so insensitive to the feelings of a child that he would embrace him in spite of the child's revulsion, and indeed not notice the child's feelings at all, is not embracing a real child but only the idea of a child, a child-object. He embraces this particular one not because he cares about it but because, since it is a blood relative, he is permitted to embrace it. If he tried to pick up and hug some strange and resisting child on the street, he might get into trouble, particularly if he was a man. For even though children are love objects, any one of us is only permitted to use physically certain children in this way.

All of this is not to say by any means that our desire to love children is bad, or all bad. We are naturally and rightly interested, charmed, and delighted by many qualities of children—their energy, enthusiasm, health, quickness, boisterousness, curiosity, intelligence, gaiety, spontaneity, vivacity, intensity, passion, expressiveness, hopefulness, trustfulness, playfulness, generosity, magnanimity, and above all their great capacity for wonder and delight. And we should be, as we often are, touched and saddened by their littleness, weakness, inexperience, ignorance, clumsiness, vulnerability, and lack of all sense of time and proportion. But we have no right to indulge these feelings, to wallow in them because they make us feel so good, or to convey them to the child by look, word, or deed unless he has given us good reason to believe that he will welcome them. When a child is feeling friendly, frolicsome, and flirtatious, this is the time to beam and smile at him, to play secret eye and smile games with him. Perhaps, if he gives us the signal, we may pick him up, tumble him about, hug and kiss him. But unless and until he gives the signal, we do not have the right.

Not long ago, at the house of her parents, a six-year-old friend of mine asked if she could read to me. I said yes, so she got a book, one she had read several times before, nestled herself in a comfortable position against me, and began.

From having read the book before, she knew the story and many of the words. But there were still quite a few that had to be puzzled out a second time. Sometimes she would make a tentative guess and ask me if it was right, which it often was. Sometimes she would simply ask me the word, in which case I would tell her.

After some time, feeling relaxed, comfortable, and affectionate, and seeing next to me the head of this child of whom I am fond, I gave it a pat. Instantly she turned to me with a look of mild surprise and question, as if to say, "What did you do that for, we're reading." I said, "Excuse me." And we continued to read.

We must learn to recognize and respect whatever distance the child has chosen to put between us. We do not have with him, any more than with anyone else, the right to move into his life space without his permission. Children don't like being used as love objects, even by people they like. They want the right to refuse, to set the terms, the ground rules, on which at any moment the relationship will proceed.

I recall a conversation I once heard between a mother and her thirteen-year-old daughter. The daughter was talking very positively about something of great importance to her. The mother, a most tactful and respectful woman, who was then, as always, very interested in anything her daughter has to say, was listening intently, commenting now and then. Suddenly the thought came to her, as she has told me it often does, "Can it really be that this remarkable young human being, holding forth here in front of me on so many topics, advancing so positively into the world, is my child? The same little person that I have been living with all these years?"

And thinking this she was overcome by a flood of fond memories and feelings. Her expression changed in a very subtle way; she looked at the daughter with a wondering amusement and tenderness. There was no condescension in it, nothing but the greatest affection; but for the moment the present child disappeared, or at the very least was joined by all the past children she had been. The daughter spotted this and realized that for the instant she was no longer there to her mother as a real person, but only as My Child. She was deeply offended and broke off her conversation. Though her mother, and I too, tried to get her to go on, the thread of contact had been broken, and she would not start talking again. But only for a short time; she knows that her mother very much respects her as a person, and in an hour or so we were conversing once more.

Most children are not as fortunate as this one. They learn early that they can be, and regularly are, commanded to give and receive tokens of love—words of endearment, simpering smiles, heavy-handed teasing, compliments and personal remarks, and hugs and kisses. This soon kills the meaning of these signs, even the hugs and the kisses, and often leaves the children without any way to express what they often feel—an affection or delight too strong for words. In time, what they are no longer able to express they may find hard even to feel. In this way we may be destroying what we most want to save. "Being affectionate" to children, "loving" them, whether they like it or not, may not be the way to make them affectionate and loving. Quite the reverse. No one can truly say "Yes" to something, be it an experience or another person's offer of love, if he cannot truly say "No." No one can wholeheartedly accept and welcome love if he does not have an unquestioned right to refuse it. No one can fully and freely give love if he does not have the unquestioned right to withhold it.

Those men who want to use, and do use, women as sex objects naturally develop a theory, an ideology, to go along with it. They justify this way of using women by inventing the notion that to be used this way is what all women really want. Thus we have the "Playboy philosophy," which proclaims that what all women really want and care about, far more than anything else, is sex. Never mind what they say or seem to feel; they really want sex. And they are insatiable. They can't have too much of it. Therefore, when a man uses them as sex objects, in fantasy or reality, it is okay, he is doing them a favor, giving them what they really want. So no need to hang back or be shy in any way, jump right in and help yourself, there can't be any such thing as too soon or too much.

Quite naturally we have an ideology very much like this to justify our using children as love objects. Children need love, the story goes. They can't have too much of it, can't get enough of it, don't care from whom or in what form it comes. All they want is love, love, love. Perhaps in the first year or so of life, there may be some truth in this. From my own and others' experience I believe that babies like and need a lot of human contact and may suffer if they get too little of it. But even with babies we must use discretion and tact. Most babies certainly like to be held, cuddled, and played with. But not necessarily all the time, or with all people, or in the same ways. By the time they are six months old, or even younger, they have their own well-developed purposes, needs, and preferences. There may be times when they are busy with something and don't want to be interrupted. There may be people they like and others they like much less or not at all. Or they may like to be played with but not picked up. And there may be certain kinds of games or ways of showing affection that they don't like from anyone. Even with babies we must take care to learn to read their signals and to respect them.

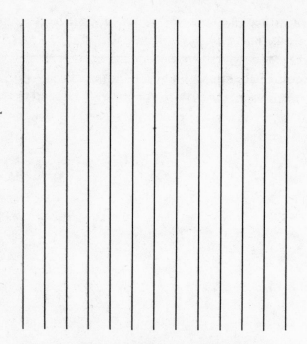

12. ON SEEING CHILDREN
AS "CUTE"

Another way of saying this is that we should try to get out of the habit of seeing little children as cute. By this I mean in part that we should try to be more aware of what it is in children to which we respond and to tell which responses are authentic, respectful, and life-enhancing and which are condescending or sentimental. Our response to a child is authentic when we are responding to qualities in the child that are not only real but valuable human qualities we would be glad to find in someone of any age. It is condescending when we respond to qualities that enable us to feel superior to the child. It is sentimental when we respond to qualities that do not exist in the child but only in some vision or theory that we have about children.

In responding to children as cute, we are in part responding to many qualities that rightly, as if by healthy instinct, appeal to us. Children tend to be, among other things, healthy, energetic, quick, vital, vivacious, enthusiastic, resourceful, intelligent, intense, passionate, hopeful, trustful, and forgiving—they get very angry but do not, like us, bear grudges for long. Above all, they have a great capacity for delight, joy, and sorrow. But we should not think of these qualities or virtues as "childish," the exclusive property of children. They are *human* qualities. We are wise to value them in people of all ages. When we think of these qualities as childish, belonging only to children, we invalidate them, make them seem things we should "outgrow" as we grow older. Thus we excuse ourselves for carelessly losing what we should have done our best to keep. Worse yet, we teach the children this lesson; most of the bright and successful ten-year-olds I have known, though they still kept the curiosity of their younger years, had learned to be ashamed of it and hide it. Only "little kids" went around all the time asking silly questions. To be grown-up was to be cool, impassive, unconcerned, untouched, invulnerable.

Perhaps women are taught to feel this way less than men; perhaps custom gives them a somewhat greater license to be childlike, which they should take care not to lose.

But though we may respond authentically to many qualities of children, we too often respond either condescendingly or sentimentally to many others—condescendingly to their littleness, weakness, clumsiness, ignorance, inexperience, incompetence, helplessness, dependency, immoderation, and lack of any sense of time or proportion; and sentimentally to made-up notions about their happiness, carefreeness, innocence, purity, nonsexuality, goodness, spirituality, and wisdom. These notions are mostly nonsense. Children are not particularly happy or carefree; they have as many worries and fears as many adults, often the same ones. What makes them seem happy is their energy and curiosity, their involvement with life; they do not waste much time in brooding. Children are the farthest thing in the world from spiritual. They are not abstract, but concrete. They are animals and sensualists; to them, what *feels* good *is* good. They are self-absorbed and selfish. They have very little ability to put themselves in another person's shoes, to imagine how he feels. This often makes them inconsiderate and sometimes cruel, but whether they are kind or cruel, generous or greedy, they are always so on impulse rather than by plan or principle. They are barbarians, primitives, about whom we are also often sentimental. Some of the things (which are not school subjects and can't be "taught") that children don't know, but only learn in time and from living, are things they will be better for knowing. Growing up and growing older are not always or only or necessarily a decline and a defeat. Some of the understanding and wisdom that can come with time is real—which is why children are attracted by the natural authority of any adults who do respond authentically and respectfully to them.

Some might ask, what is wrong with responding sentimentally to children, with thinking them better than they really are. How can we think too much good of someone? What harm can it do? Many years ago I found in a bookstore in London a secondhand paperback copy of a book called *Novel on Yellow Paper* by Stevie Smith. It became, and has

remained, one of my favorites. Reading it recently, and looking for a particular passage, I came across a paragraph that I
had completely forgotten. When I had first read it, it did
not touch any of my concerns and went by unnoticed. This
time it struck like a blow. It says, as eloquently as anything
I have ever read, what I am here trying to say about looking
on children as cute and exploiting their cuteness and how
this sentimental and therefore abstract and unreal way of
dealing with children is so near always to callousness and
cruelty.

> . . . (when I was eight years old) there was a maid there that
> took a fancy to me. She used to sit me on her knee. If I was
> in the mood for it I could play up to her fancy, but even
> while I was doing this I was immensely terrified. Her feeling
> for me, I felt this very keenly but could not for some time
> understand why it so much dismayed me, was in outward
> appearance, so far as being hugged and set on her knee, was
> what in outward appearance my mother . . . ? No, do you
> see, but it was profoundly disturbing, how in essence her
> feeling was so arbitrary, so superficial, so fortuituous. And
> so this feeling she had for me, which was not at all a deep
> feeling, but as one might pet, pat, and cuddle a puppy,
> filled me with the fear that a child has in the face of cruelty.
> It was so insecure, so without depth or significance. It was
> so similar in outward form, and so asunder and apart, so
> deceitful and so barbarous in significance. It is very pro-
> foundly disturbed and dismayed and terrified me.

One afternoon I was with several hundred people in an
auditorium of a junior college when we heard outside the
building the passionate wail of a small child. Almost everyone smiled, chuckled, or laughed. Perhaps there was something legitimately comic in the fact that one child should,

without even trying, be able to interrupt the supposedly important thoughts and words of all these adults. But beyond this was something else, the belief that the feelings, pains, and passions of children were not *real*, not to be taken seriously. If we had heard outside the building the voice of an adult crying in pain, anger, or sorrow, we would not have smiled or laughed but would have been frozen in wonder and terror. Most of the time, when it is not an unwanted distraction, or a nuisance, the crying of children strikes us as funny. We think, there they go again, isn't it something the way children cry, they cry about almost anything. But there is nothing funny about children's crying. Until he has learned from adults to exploit his childishness and cuteness, a small child does not cry for trivial reasons but out of need, fear, or pain.

Once, coming into an airport, I saw just ahead of me a girl of about seven or eight. Hurrying up the carpeted ramp, she tripped and fell down. She did not hurt herself but quickly picked herself up and walked on. But looking around on everyone's face I saw indulgent smiles, expressions of "isn't that cute?" They would not have thought it funny or cute if an adult had fallen down but would have worried about his pain and embarrassment.

The trouble with sentimentality, and the reason why it always leads to callousness and cruelty, is that it is abstract and unreal. We look at the lives and concerns and troubles of children as we might look at actors on a stage, a comedy as long as it does not become a nuisance. And so, since their feelings and their pain are neither serious nor real, any pain we may cause them is not real either. In any conflict of interest with us, they must give way; only our needs are real. Thus when an adult wants for his own pleasure to hug and kiss a child for whom his embrace is unpleasant or terrifying, we easily say that the child's unreal feelings don't count, it is only the adult's real needs that count. People who treat children like living dolls when they are feeling good may treat them like unliving dolls—fling them into a corner or throw them downstairs or out of the window—when they are feeling bad. "Little angels" quickly become "little devils."

Even in those happy families in which the children are not jealous of each other, not competing for a scarce supply of attention and approval, but are more or less good friends, they don't think of each other as cute and are not sentimental about children littler than they are. Bigger children in happy families may be very tender and careful toward the little ones. But such older children do not tell themselves and would not believe stories about the purity and goodness of the smaller child. They know very well that the young child is littler, clumsier, more ignorant, more in need of help, and much of the time more unreasonable and troublesome. Because children do not think of each other as cute, they often seem to be harder on each other than we think we would be. They are blunt and unsparing. But on the whole this frankness, which accepts the other as a complete person, even if one not always or altogether admired, is less harmful to the children than the way many adults deal with them.

Much of what we respond to in children as cute is not strength or virtue, real or imagined, but weakness, a quality which gives us power over them or helps us to feel superior. Thus we think they are cute partly because they are little. But what is cute about being little? Are midgets cute? Not at all; we recognize that the littleness of a midget is an affliction and burden. Children understand this very well. They are not at all sentimental about their own littleness. They would rather be big than little, and they want to get big as soon as they can.

How would we feel about children, react to them, deal with them, if they reached their full size in the first two or three years of their lives? We would not be able to go on using them as love objects or slaves or property. We would have no interest in keeping them helpless, dependent, baby-ish. Since they were grown-up physically, we would want them to grow up in other ways. On their part, they would want to become free, active, independent, and responsible as fast as they could, and since they were full-sized and could not be used any longer as living dolls or super-pets we would do all we could do to help them do so.

Or suppose that people varied in size as much as dogs, with normal adults anywhere from one foot to seven feet tall. We would not then think of the littleness of children as something that was cute. It would simply be a condition, like being bald or hairy, fat or thin. That someone was little would not be a signal for us to experience certain feelings or make important judgements about his character or the kinds of relationships we might have with him.

Another quality of children that makes us think they are cute, makes us smile or get misty-eyed, is their "innocence." What do we mean by this? In part we mean only that they are ignorant and inexperienced. But ignorance is not a bless-ing, it is a misfortune. Children are no more sentimental about their ignorance than they are about their size. They want to escape their ignorance, to know what's going on, and we should be glad to help them escape it if they ask us and if we can. But by the innocence of children we mean some-thing more—their hopefulness, trustfulness, confidence, their feeling that the world is open to them, that life has many possibilities, that what they don't know they can find out, what they can't do they can learn to do. These are qualities valuable in everyone. When we call them "innocence" and ascribe them only to children, as if they were too dumb to know any better, we are only trying to excuse our own hopelessness and despair.

Today in the Boston Public Garden I watched, as I often do, some infants who were just learning to walk. I used to think their clumsiness, their uncertain balance and wandering course, were cute. Now I tried to watch in a different spirit. For there is nothing cute about clumsiness, any more than littleness. Any adult who found it as hard to walk as a small child, and who did it so badly, would be called severely handicapped. We certainly would not smile, chuckle, and laugh at his efforts—and congratulate ourselves for doing so. Watching the children, I thought of this. And I reminded myself, as I often do when I see a very small child intent and absorbed in what he is doing and I am tempted to think of him as cute, "That child isn't trying to be cute; he doesn't see himself as cute; and he doesn't want to be seen as cute. He is as serious about what he is doing now as any human being can be, and he wants to be taken seriously."

But there is something very appealing and exciting about watching children just learning to walk. They do it so badly, it is so clearly difficult, and in the child's terms may even be dangerous. *We* know it won't hurt him to fall down, but he can't be sure of that and in any case doesn't like it. Most adults, even many older children, would instantly stop trying to do anything that they did as badly as a new walker does his walking. But the infant keeps on. He is so determined, he is working so hard, and he is so excited; his learning to walk is not just an effort and struggle but a joyous adventure. As I watch this adventure, no less a miracle be-cause we all did it, I try to respond to the child's determina-tion, courage, and pleasure, not his littleness, feebleness, and incompetence. To whatever voice in me says, "Oh, wouldn't it be nice to pick up that dear little child and give him a big hug and kiss," I reply, "No, no, NO, that child doesn't want to be picked up, hugged, and kissed, he wants to *walk*. He doesn't know or care whether I like it or not, he is not walk-ing for the approval or happiness of me or even for his par-ents beside him, but for himself. It is his show. Don't try to turn him into an actor in your show. Leave him alone to get on with his work."

We often think children are most cute when they are most intent and serious about what they are doing. In our minds we say to the child, "You think that what you are doing is important; we know it's not; like everything else in your life that you take seriously, it is trivial." We smile ten-derly at the child carefully patting his mud pie. We feel that mud pie is not serious and all the work he is putting into it is a waste (though we may tell him in a honey-dearie voice that it is a *beautiful* mud pie). But he doesn't know that; in his ignorance he is just as serious as if he were doing some-thing important. How satisfying for us to feel we know better.

We tend to think that children are most cute when they are openly displaying their ignorance and incompetence. We value their dependency and helplessness. They are help ob-jects as well as love objects. Children acting really compe-tently and intelligently do not usually strike us as cute. They are as likely to puzzle and threaten us. We don't like to see a child acting in a way that makes it impossible for us to look down on him or to suppose that he depends on our help.

This is of course very true in school. The child whose teachers know that he knows things they don't know may be in trouble. We know, too, how much schools and first-grade teachers hate to have children come to school already knowing how to read. How then will the school teach him? When we see a young child doing anything very well, we are likely to think there is something wrong with him. He is too precocious, he is peculiar, he is going to have troubles someday, he is "acting like an adult," he has "lost his childhood." Many people reacted so to the extraordinarily capable child pupils of the Japanese violin teacher Suzuki. And I remember the sociologist Omar K. Moore telling me that when he first showed that many three-year-olds, given certain kinds of typewriters and equipment to use and experiment with, could very quickly teach themselves to read (which they weren't supposed to have the visual acuity, coordination, or mental ability to do), he received a flood of indignant and angry letters accusing him of mistreating the children.

Children do not like being incompetent any more than they like being ignorant. They want to learn how to do, and do well, the things they see being done by bigger people around them. This is why they soon find school such a disappointment; they so seldom get a chance to learn anything important or do anything real. But many of the defenders of childhood, in or out of school, seem to have this vested interest in the children's incompetence, which they often call "letting the child be a child."

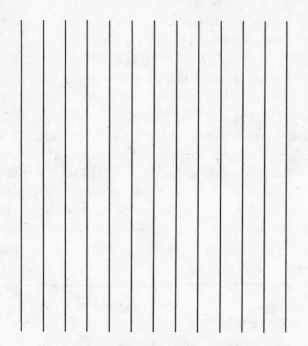

13. HOW CHILDREN EXPLOIT CUTENESS

A man once said to me, "I have two small children, and I think they're cute, and I still don't see what harm there is in it." I said that perhaps, despite his thinking of them as cute, the way in which he lived, talked, and dealt with his children might in fact do no harm. Without seeing him and his children together, I could not tell. But this habit of seeing them as cute had great dangers in it.

For one thing it tended to make him see them abstractly. This abstractness is the enemy of true understanding, sympathy, or love.

When one person sees and deals with another not as a unique person but as an example of a type, whether Celebrity, Black, Sex Symbol, Great Genius, Artist, Saint, or whatever, he diminishes that person and makes it hard for any natural relationship to grow between them. This is what we do to children when we see them as Cute, Adorable, Innocent. For the real child before us we substitute some idea of Childhood that we have in our minds and deal with that. Often, when we label someone in this way, we invest him with magical properties, sometimes bad, sometimes good.

In a society that worships physical beauty, as ours does, we make many of these magical assumptions about people solely on the basis of how they look. Men often do this to women they consider beautiful. The young man, seeing a Pretty Girl, assumes that she is smarter, funnier, more gentle, loving, passionate—in a word, more Perfect—than others who look less striking. The opposite may well be true; great beauty is as likely to hurt as to help a woman's character. If the young man manages to enter into some kind of love relationship with the Pretty Girl, and finds that she is no more Perfect than anyone else, he may feel disappointed and deceived, may cry out in pain, "I believed you were better than other people, how could you betray my hopes!"

Not long ago the magazine *Psychology Today* published the results of a study in which people were shown a number of photographs of strangers and asked what they thought about various facets of their characters. (If any of the people tested said that this request was ridiculous, as it is, the article did not mention it.) As we might have expected, people made much more favorable assumptions about the strangers who were most conventionally good-looking. Other tests and long experience have shown this to be very true of teachers; they generally think the most handsome children are brighter, more talented, better behaved, natural leaders. From such children they expect much more. They also forgive much more; as every school child knows, a cute-looking child gets away with much more than a homely one.

Having turned the child into an ideal abstraction, many parents and teachers tend to look at him much as Rocket Control in Houston looks at a moon shot. They have a trajectory (life) all mapped out for this child, and they are constantly monitoring him to see whether he is on the path or whether he needs a little boost from this rocket (psychologist) here or a sideways push from that rocket (learning specialist) there. Is he on course? Is he on schedule? Is he in the correct attitude?

Others say this young person must be seen and understood for what he does, thinks, and feels now. To the extent that this is what people mean who say, "Kids are not potential adults, they are kids" mean this, I agree. Unfortunately many defenders of childhood usually mean much more than that. They have their own precise notions of what a child should be. They tend to slip very easily into the condescending sentimentality I have described. They are very often the same people who like to tell us that children are more wise, beautiful, "human" (a favorite word), happy, virtuous, pure, and sane than adults. Such talk is very discouraging or damaging to the young. No one who is small, powerless, ignorant, anxious, and confused wants to be told that this is the best time of his life.

As I write this, I have just walked through the Boston Public Garden on a sunny April morning. There I saw many mothers out with small children, many of them what we call toddlers. Watching their eagerness and energy, and sharing their pleasure in the world around them, I thought, if Nature had made a creature which was exactly like a healthy and confident three- or four-year-old child for its entire lifetime, it would make the world's finest pet, not as active or graceful as some other animals, perhaps, but far more intelligent and trainable and able to please and delight us in many more ways. If there were such permanently childlike super-pets, there would be no reason not to treat them as such. But little children are not going to remain three years old, soft, cute, cuddly, dependent. They have a life ahead of them, in which they will be a great many persons. And we have no right, early in their lives, to treat them in a way that will diminish or injure any of those other persons they will become. The saying "kids are kids, not potential adults" cuts two ways. It can lead us out of one mistake and into another just as bad. For the child is a "kid" *and* a potential adult. Certainly, we have no right to treat him *as if nothing but the present person would ever exist.* If it is wrong—I agree that it is—to think of him only in terms of his future, it is just as wrong to think of him as if he had no future.

Back in the late 1940s, someone wrote a science fiction story about childlike pets, which he called Neutroids. In a world so overpopulated that governments could only allow a few children to be born, these Neutroids had been bred or created by scientists to comfort all those people who felt they needed and wanted children, *i.e.,* some childlike love object. It now seems to me as if many of those who say we should not treat children as potential adults—potential doctors or lawyers or businessmen—are only urging us to treat them as Neutroids instead. This seems as bad if not worse.

When we have preconceived ideas about the young, whether we see them as potential successful adults or as Innocent Spirits (Neutroids), we inevitably begin to judge them by how well they fit into these ideas. When they play the parts we have written for them, we are pleased; when they do not, we are worried, disappointed, or angry. It is easy to condemn this when it is done by people who are ambitious for their children, who want to push them into success so that they may take credit for it and so justify their own lives. But this judging of children against an abstract ideal is done just as much, though in a different way, by the people who think children are cute.

When we think that children are cute we tend to use their cuteness to arouse in ourselves feelings which give us pleasure and which make us feel proud for having them. This alone would be bad enough. But this exploitation of the child becomes mutual. As we exploit him, we teach him to exploit us. We exploit his cuteness; he exploits our need to have him behave cutely. He learns when very young that when he behaves towards us in certain ways we are pleased and when he does not we are hurt or angry. If this were only a matter of such behavior as eating his food or not breaking things or pulling the kitten's tail, there would be no harm in it. Usually it is not that simple. The child senses that we want something from him but is not sure what it is. If he is very strong and independent, he may not give the matter much more thought. Otherwise he will begin to try to find out how to play this game the adults want him to join in playing.

What the adult wants, of course, is to use this child as love object, to have him act out the part of Ideal Cute Child. Often he may want even more. The person who says how much he loves children may only and really be saying how much he needs to be loved *by* children, may want from them the kind of uncritical, undemanding, unconditional, total love a baby wants from its mother. He may want to reverse the roles, make himself the child and the children his parents, have them give him what no one else has ever given him. He may seek in children the ideal lover of his dreams.

A subtle power struggle may then begin. As he figures out what the adult wants, the child may decide to give it to him then and there and get his reward. Or he may decide to hold out, to refuse to give the adult what he wants, in order to see what happens next. He begins to tease and coquette. More often than not, the adult, if his need to use the cute child as love object is great, will begin to plead, cajole, tempt, bargain, and even threaten. The child soon learns that the longer he holds out, the greater his rewards will be, at least up to the point where the now disappointed and angry adult refuses to play any longer. How far can he push this point? How long can he hold out on the adult who wants him to smile at him, play games with him, sit on his lap, give him a kiss? Much of this calculating and game-playing is unconscious, goes on at various emotional or gut levels. But if it goes on very long, if the child cannot escape from these games, these mutual exploitations of need, they will surely destroy his character.

Such a cute child soon learns to do almost everything he does, at least around adults, to get an effect. He becomes self-conscious, artful, calculating, manipulative. He pays more and more attention to how he appears in the eyes of others, becomes more and more concerned with others' opinions of him. In the excellent phrase of Erich Fromm, he takes on a marketing orientation. He sells his behavior, his personality, and himself for rewards which, like the praise junkies we make in school, he comes more and more to depend on. But

many a child learns these tricks long before he goes to school
—I often see such simpering, mincing, cutesy-smiling, fake-
laughing children with adults in public places. He becomes a
specialist in human relations, which he sees more and more
as a kind of contest to see who can get the most out of the
other.

A ten-year-old in my class had grown up this way. People told me that when she was smaller she used to go to one
of those "dancing schools" where they dress the small children up in costumes and have them perform for the adults.
Just the other day I read about one of those places in a story
in the *Boston Globe* about Art Linkletter's "Young World":

> . . . [the Director] walks over to the gallery of framed
> photographs on the wall behind his desk. He points out each
> picture and tells the stories behind the photographs of "our
> girls" in their frills and feathers and sequins, performing
> during various dance recitals.
> "Our girls have confidence because we treat them with con-
> stant love and kindness. All of our dance teachers do this.
> I like to pat their heads, pinch their cheeks, pull their ears.
> They really melt me, the little angels," he says. "Give me a
> woman who says, 'What can I do for my little girl' and I
> can take that little girl, especially if she's shy, and put her
> on stage in front of 1,000 people, and she'll sing like a bird,
> without hesitation. And she'll sing so sweetly and move so
> gracefully that her mother, her father, her teacher, and even
> her director will cry." [My note: Nothing in the story as it
> appeared gave the slightest hint that the writer saw in the
> above anything to criticize or question—the general tone of
> the story was approving.]

This child in my class, when younger, had apparently
been very pretty. All the teachers who had taught her in our

school assured me that she was adorable and that I would just love her. She proved to be by all odds the most unhappy, angry, disagreeable, self-hating, and self-destructive child of that age I have ever known. Much of the time she tried to boss the other children around at the top of her voice. When they grew tired of this and would not stand for it any longer, refused to do what she ordered, or ignored her, she would pout, sulk, and usually cry. As I knew her better it seemed more and more clear that in all her life she had never known any relationships with people that were not mutually exploitive. While the adults, dance directors, parents, exploited her littleness and cuteness to get warm feelings and misty eyes, she used these same qualities to get out of the adults whatever she wanted. She knew no way of dealing with other people except seduction, and when that failed, tears and rage. Now that she was no longer cute, but had become a sugar addict, fat, lazy, and inactive, seduction failed more and more. But she had nothing else. Seduction was all she knew.

What kind of adults will such children become? What kind of society will they make? What will they do to satisfy their insatiable craving for the approval of other people?

Many people call such artful, affected, seductive behavior "babyish." This is a terrible libel on babies. Babies are not "babyish." Up to the age of a year, at least, they are intensely serious. They like to laugh but when not laughing they are on the whole solemn, frank, and direct. They are not connivers, seducers, tricksters. We might well say that, in spite of their littleness and helplessness, babies act more grown up, in the best sense, than they will a few years later. They have to learn to act "babyish." Some learn it at home, some in school. A mother discussing this with me said, as many mothers have, that her child never picked up this sort of artificial, affected, silly behavior until she went to school. She saw the other children do it, saw that it worked with most teachers, and was often anxious enough to feel she needed to do it herself. A few children have the integrity and courage not to give in. They are often labeled stubborn, defiant, troublemakers. Most of them soon fall in line.

The generally bright and capable middle-class first-graders that I taught had all, boys and girls, learned to use this "babyish" behavior as a way of dealing with and fooling the adults, getting out of trouble, getting what they wanted. Whenever they felt under some sort of pressure from me, when they hadn't done some work, or didn't know what I wanted, or didn't think they could do what I wanted, they would begin to walk with little mincing steps, their voices would go high and whiny, they would talk a kind of semi-babytalk. Fortunately, it didn't take them long to learn that there was nothing I liked less, that this was the worst possible tactic to use with me. They quickly gave it up—except, now and then, to tease me.

To sum up, when we think of children as cute we abstract and idealize them, judge them, exploit them, and, worst of all, teach them to exploit us and each other, to sell themselves for smiles and rewards. This is in every way bad for them and for their relations with us.

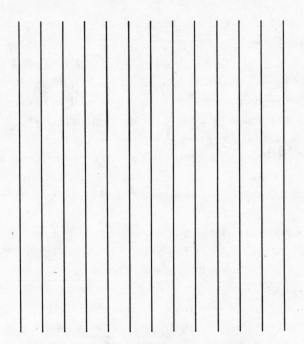

14. LOVE MAY NOT CURE EVERYTHING

Even those places where the children have a good deal of the control of their own lives—schools, camps, playgrounds—often have trouble with a particular kind of child, the kind who is always irritating, teasing, picking on people, testing, bullying, hurting. George Dennison in *The Lives Of Children* wrote about one such child at the First Street School. His name was Stanley, he was about twelve, he had made and been in constant trouble everywhere he had been, and the authorities told the teachers at First Street School that if Stanley couldn't make it there, there was nothing left for him but some sort of jail. The other children at the school begged the adults not to let him in, said he would wreck the place. The adults let him in, hoping that they might be able to help him. But the children were right; the school could not give the help he needed (if that was what he needed), and before they finally got tough-minded enough to tell him to leave, he almost did wreck the place.

Herb Snitzer, in his book *Today Is for Children, Numbers Can Wait,* tells of four such troublemakers he had at the Lewis-Wadhams School—Steve, Donald, Tim, and Jason. Steve was the unloved and unwanted fat boy, self-appointed butt of everyone's jokes, and like all such, the maker of mean jokes at others' expense. Donald was the hard-driven child of anxious parents, very bright, small, by his acts always driving away the affection and approval he wanted and needed, always trying to make up for his lack of what Erich Fromm calls "potency" by dominating others. Tim was a gangling, unattractive awkward boy, with " . . . an enormously practical-minded mother, three older sisters, and a father who was absent most of the time, even when he was present—an imaginative, highly successful and committed scientist and the epitome of the absent-minded professor." Tim was, in short, a good example of Erik Erikson's observation that many young people would rather be something bad, or even dead, than feel they were nothing. And Jason, leader of the gang of six terrorists—well, we never find out what was eating Jason. But in every way he could he made the other children's lives miserable. Here the children talk about him and the other bullies at a school meeting:

> I think bullying is making other people the scapegoat just so the scapegoat won't be you.

Why does there have to be a scapegoat?

Well, like a lot of us, maybe before they came here those boys who bully us got scapegoated somewhere else and think they would be here too.

If they don't think anyone cares about them . . .

How are you supposed to care about someone who's beating up on you all the time or threatening you?

Well, you can pretend to. Like you hang around and laugh when they beat up on someone else or make them cry or something. If you act like you're on their side, then you think it won't be you next time.

I just run when I see one coming. (A little kid.)

Laughter. Then indignation:

I don't see what's funny about it. To me its sad. Sad for the bullies, I mean. People pretend to like them so they won't get hurt, or run and hide or keep very still and hope not to be noticed. I think that's sad. What if they knew we really wanted to like them? Wouldn't that help more?

Well, they are part of the community, after all.

I don't really not like them.

What we're really all trying to say, I think, is that we do care about them and they shouldn't think we only care about us. We really care about them too, and that's why we're having this meeting, to try to help, so wouldn't that help, just knowing that, I mean. . . . [P. 142]

This is a far more understanding and forgiving attitude toward wrongdoing than we would be likely to find in most older people. On the other hand, the students did vote later in the year to expel Jason. What was Jason's response to the concern of his fellow students? He said that what he really wanted was to hit Herb Snitzer as hard as he could and that if he could do that, could really hurt him, maybe he could stop bullying.

Some years ago a friend of mine, Claud Crawford, was principal of a public elementary school in Douglas, Michigan, and the head of a program, successful until an organized right-wing minority ended it, which joined in one school quite traditional and quite open classes. He told me about a boy in the fifth grade. This boy was poor; he and his family had recently come to Michigan from Applachia. Also, since he was not a successful student and had had to drop back a year or more in his schooling, he was the oldest and the biggest kid in the grade. Almost as soon as he entered the class he became the chief bully and troublemaker. All the other children disliked and feared him. For a while the teacher did what she could about this, but soon she began to send the boy to the principal. After a number of talks Crawford was able to persuade the boy that the reason the other kids didn't like him and didn't want anything to do with him might not be that he was poor or talked differently but simply that he was so mean to them. If he began to try instead to be more helpful and friendly, perhaps many of the other children might begin to be friendly in return. The boy said he would give it a try. For a while things improved, there were no more trips to the office, and the teacher said how much better he was getting on with the other children. Then, after about a month or so, the boy began to backslide, to pick on the others. Soon he was back in the office. Crawford said to him, "I thought you had decided to try to get along with the other children, and make friends with them, and it was going along fine. Now it looks as if you have decided to go back to the old pattern of being everyone's enemy. Is that true?" The boy said yes. Crawford asked why. The boy thought for a while. Then he said, "It's safer this way."

There may have been more to this story than I know, or perhaps even Crawford knew. Perhaps in trying to make friends with the other children this boy met obstacles he could not cross and could not believe he would ever cross. Perhaps, as he knew the other children better, he (and they) realized more and more in how many ways he really was different—and children, like the rest of us, don't like things to be very different. Perhaps he became more aware and more ashamed of his poverty. Perhaps the other children's parents told them that they did not think this big poor kid was a proper playmate. Perhaps, with the bitter wisdom of poverty and experience, the boy saw that as he got older the gulf between him and the others would grow not narrower but wider. Or perhaps if only he had had more patience and confidence things would have worked out all right.

What is clear, though, is that this boy fell back on the strategy of deliberate failure, which so many children, and older people, in and out of schools, use to protect themselves from the disappointment, humiliation, shame, and pain of not being able to do what they had set out to do. This boy, wise for his years, and perhaps like the bullies at Lewis-Wadhams and many other places, saw rightly that it was safer to do what he knew he could do—make enemies, make people hate and fear him—than to try to do what he had never done, did not know he could do, and had no reason to believe he could do—make friends, make people like and trust him.

At Summerhill in the spring of 1965, at a General School Meeting, a boy of about eight brought up another boy

135

of about eleven for bullying. He said that the older one was always picking on him, following him around, teasing him, insulting him, pushing him, hitting him. The older boy was standing against a wall, somewhat aside from the general mass of the meeting. The chairman asked him if the younger boy's report was true. The older boy did not deny it. The chairman then said, "How come you keep picking on this kid? You've been brought up before?" Other voices chimed in, "Yes, how come?" The older boy muttered something about the younger kid driving him crazy. Half a dozen voices then said, "Okay, then stay away from him. He doesn't follow you around. Just keep out of his way if the sight of him annoys you so much." Then someone pointed out that since this had come up before, many times, they had to find some new way to discourage this bully. Various punishments were proposed, and wisely rejected, as being likely to do more harm than good. Finally it was decided that the next time the bigger boy picked on the smaller, the smaller could instantly call a General School Meeting to take up the matter. Whether this stopped the bullying, I never knew. At the time it seemed that the school had found a humane and sensible way to deal with the problem. Now I am less sure. It seems at least possible that the bully, the center of everyone's attention and the object of everyone's concern, was, whether he knew it or not, getting not punishment but something that he wanted, something that he bullied in order to get. Attention, yes, certainly that. But also much more than that.

These destructive people, these Stanleys and Steves and Jasons, tell themselves: I am no good; nobody can possibly like me; if I try to make friends I will be rejected and will look like a fool; therefore, I won't try, I'll spare myself the disappointment and pain of failure; and what's more I'll deny them the satisfaction of rejecting me; I'll let them see that I don't think their friendship is even worth having; and since whatever I do these people are going to turn against me sooner or later I'll pay them back in advance and give them as hard a time as I can. And so the policy of protective deliberate failure turns into a policy of spite. These self-haters go on to think: the only way I can assert myself, keep some shred of self-esteem, is by frustrating all the attempts of these people to "help" me—which only shows again that they think they are so much better than I am. And so the bad kid, brought up once more for discussion in the school meeting (what *can* we do to help Jason?) is getting what he wants or at least what he wants most among all the things he thinks he has any chance to get. He has turned the tables. Instead of his pleading with everyone else, Love me! Please love me!, they are pleading with him, How can we help you? How can we make you believe we care about you? Instead of his begging the others for what they have the power to deny, the others are begging and he—the unyielding, the haughty, the Proud Prince—is withholding, denying, rejecting. It is like the fantasy of the rejected lover, who daydreams with bitter pleasure of the loved one coming to him pleading to be accepted and himself sadly but sternly rejecting these pleas saying, "No, you had your chance, now it's too late." This is the daydream that these people are acting out in the meeting. Every time they get in trouble they get a new chance to play this great part. It is the only power and comfort they have.

What we should understand is that it is possible to fail as completely at a free or alternative school like Summerhill or Lewis-Wadhams or First Street School as at the most rigid and conventional school. In a school whose main work is having everyone get good marks on exams, whoever can't do this is a failure. But in a school whose main work is helping everyone to be happy, to love and be loved, anyone who can't do *this* is just as much a failure. And the shame and pain of such failure may be even greater, because the student really shares the aims of the school, really wants to be a success at love and happiness, and knows that everyone is really trying to help him and that when he fails he has only himself to blame.

There may be no way to make children like Tim, Jason, Donald, and Steve feel lovable. What we might do is give them access to experiences in which at least for a little while they might forget whether they are lovable or not.

The best talk to a graduating class I have ever heard or read, and perhaps the only really good one, was given by Dean Paul Roberts of Denver at the first graduation of the Colorado Rocky Mountain School. To a group of students that included some very unhappy, mixed-up, and self-hating young people, he said: (1) accept yourself, (2) forget yourself, (3) find something to do and to care about that is more important to you than you are. All perhaps conventional enough, the sort of talk young people hear with a yawn. But what from many adults might have sounded like old cliches, boring preachy grown-up talk, in this case came over as truth. In telling the students to accept and then to forget themselves Dean Roberts was saying something that they, preoccupied, obsessed as they were by how they looked to others, and usually how bad they looked, had to take seriously. For he was one of the homeliest people any of us had ever seen. Only on faces badly disfigured by injury or disease, faces that had to be put slowly together by surgeons, could one find features so misshapen. And the fact was that Dean Roberts had so fully accepted and forgotten his extraordinary ugliness that after only a few minutes in his company you forgot it yourself and saw only a serene, kindly, friendly man. Early in his talk he told a joke on himself, with such good humor and such complete absence of any appeal for sympathy, that all of us could only laugh wholeheartedly *with* him, without any nervousness at all. He said that there was a saying in Denver that you could be sure that Paul Roberts wasn't two-faced, because if he had two faces he wouldn't be wearing the one he's got. As he told it, it was very funny, and coming from this man who was ugly beyond the wildest nightmares of any of the self-hating and self-despising students, it made his words mean a great deal.

Of course, to accept and forget oneself is not easy to do even when one tries, which is why the other part of his advice is so vital—to find something to do, to care about, to throw yourself into, that is more important than you are. I came into my twenties feeling on the whole that I was not much loved or liked and did not deserve to be. There was very little about myself that I liked and much that I did not like at all. What helped me grow out of this was not people sitting around telling me that I was okay and that they loved me. Instead I had the good luck and perhaps some saving instinct to find work that took all my energy and skill and attention, work that had to be done well and that was important, not just to me but to many other people. My first work was as an officer on a submarine, the *U.S.S. Barbero* (SS317), in World War II. The second was working for the movement for world federal government in the six years

139

after the war. In both cases, the second even more than the first, working with a great many people on something that seemed to us of immense importance, into which we put all our talent and energy, I forgot myself. At least, I forgot the "self" I had grown up with and learned to dislike. For six years I traveled, met many people, spent time with them, talked and wrote about world government, what it might mean, how we might get it, how we might persuade others to join us in working for it. We talked about the local chapters that they were all busy starting or running, how to raise money, hold better meetings, find more members, get more publicity, reach more people. And as I talked and worked and lived with these people, I gradually became aware that we had become friends, close friends, that they actually *liked* me. Later, hearing Dean Roberts' advice, I became aware that I had followed it without knowing it. For I did not go into submarines or the world government to solve my personal problems. I did the work I did because it seemed worth doing.

This is, of course, part of the problem for our unhappy young. There is, or at least seems to be, so little work in society that is worth doing, into which one might with good conscience put all one's energy. Most of the work people seem to be doing around us is monotonous, undemanding, boring, and stupid, if not actually dishonest or destructive. The good causes we know all seem like losing causes, and it doesn't help anyone who already feels like a loser to work with other losers and to keep on losing. The work for world government was exciting to me and worth all the effort I put into it because, for a number of years at least, we believed that if we did our work right we had a chance of getting world government.

What these unhappy and destructive young people may really need is not a chance to relive their unhappy childhoods but a chance to get away from them and live some other sort of life altogether. They may need, not a smaller, more protected world to live in but a bigger one. Perhaps, like all of us, they may now and then need a very small and safe world in which they can hide, rest, and regain some of their strength and courage. But this refuge, this small protected world, is only for once in a while. Most of the time, the unhappy person, young or old, needs a world big enough so that he may find there something to do that will make it possible for him to accept and forget himself.

A boy I know quite well went to a small school, not quite as relaxed and kindly as Lewis-Wadhams or Summerhill, but still not a bad place. At the ages of ten, eleven, and twelve, he was not happy there. Anxious and well-meaning adults constantly hovered around him, asking implicitly or directly what was the matter and what they could do to help. This did not make him feel any better. It made him want with desperate urgency to find a place, some kind of living space, in which people would be too busy doing whatever they were doing to give a damn whether he was happy or not. If they could forget or ignore his unhappiness, he might be able to.

Many young people, above all many unhappy ones, want and need a chance to help, to feel, in Peter Marin's words, "alive, useful, and needed." Lynn Converse, who with Peggy Hughes helped to start an adventure-junk-construction playground in Charlestown (part of Boston), told me about some of the children with whom she has been working after school hours in an empty apartment in a housing project. Her group of children has its bullies and troublemakers. But she said that the worst of these, two strong, lively, bright, and impossible eight- or nine-year-olds, are helpful and cooperative and happy whenever they have a chance to help her with some real and hard work. It has to be real and hard—it can't be a project cooked up to amuse them or keep them out of trouble and it can't be something that she could easily do without help. But if she has something heavy to move or bring in or work to do that takes skill and energy, these boys work hard, intelligently, and tirelessly until the job is done, after which they rest a while and then go back to making trouble.

A fresh start in a new place. This is what we all want, when things are not going well. Young children, when they are trying to do something and it isn't going well, say, "Wait!" Who are they saying it to? They are saying it to Time, saying, turn back, give me another chance. I think of the moment in my own life when I felt most vividly that Time and Circumstances were giving me another chance. After college, which I had not liked much, I had gone for three months to submarine school in Key West, which I liked even less. The three months over, I went to New London, Connecticut, to report to the Submarine Officer's School. It was a beautiful fall evening, clear and cool. As we walked up a hill toward the Bachelor Officers' Quarters, I felt an extraordinary sense of adventure and hope, a new life ahead. Not that I supposed that from now on I would be master of every situation. But there was this overwhelming feeling of a second chance, above all the chance to move into a world in which people didn't know me and so had no fixed ideas about me. This, much more than a lived-over childhood, or even love, may be what many unhappy young people need.

15. WHAT CHILDREN NEED, WE ALL NEED

People who feel that they understand children and want to defend them often speak about them in a way that I used to agree with but now find more and more often confused, sentimental, or misleading. They tell us that a child needs "to be allowed to be a child" or "the freedom to be a child" or "to experience childhood." They say that a child needs "time to grow" or that he should live in a "child's world" so that he may experience himself as "a human being in his own right." They speak of people trying to "destroy childhood" or "take childhood away from children."

What is wrong with such words and ideas is that much of what they imply about children and childhood is not true, and what is true applies just as much to adults as to children. To whatever extent children really need what these words say they need, so do all the rest of us, young or old. To whatever extent we adults are denied those needs by the society and culture in which we live, so must children be denied them. When we say of children's needs, as of their virtues, that they belong only to children, we make them seem trivial, we invalidate them. What is more important, we insure that they will not be met. For no amount of sentimentalizing or preaching will make a society provide for its young people a better quality of life than it provides for its adults. We fool ourselves if we think ways can be found to give children what all the rest of us so sorely lack.

"A child's world." "To experience childhood." "To be allowed to be a child." Such words seem to say that childhood is a time and an experience very different from the rest of life and that it is, or ought to be, the best part of our lives. It is not, and no one knows it better than children. *Children want to grow up.* While they are growing up, they want, some of the time, to be around the kind of adults who like being grown-up and who think of growing up as an exploration and adventure, not the process of being chased out of some garden of Eden. They do not want to hear older people say, as many people in the alternative school movement so often do, "These are the best years of your life; we are going to save them for you and keep the wicked world from spoiling them." What could be more discouraging? For they are going to grow up, whether they want to or not. They would like to think that this is something to look forward to. What they want to hear from the older people is that it gets better later. They want the kind of message my best friend sent me on my thirtieth birthday: "The best is yet to come." He was right, it was, and I still feel that way.

Young people in their late teens or early twenties have often told me that when they get out of school they want "to work with kids." If I ask why, they say things like, "Because kids are so honest, so open, so loving, because with kids you can be yourself, you don't have to lie or cheat or pretend, you can let your true self and your feelings show." In short, you can be like a child yourself. But this is not what it is like to be a child, even among other children, and many children are not like this at all. Some five-year-olds and younger, as much as any adult, are up-tight, guarded, devious, calculating, afraid to show what they feel, manipulators and con men who do almost everything they do, including smile and laugh, to get an effect or reward. First grade, even kindergarten, like any other human society, has its pecking order, its in-groups and out-groups, its anxieties, its lonely people craving affection, trying to make others like them or to understand why they don't. The social life of children, even very young ones, is not so different from that of older people. "The child's world" is not a paradise.

In spite of this, the company of young children can be very interesting, invigorating, and refreshing, as well as exhausting. It is not hard to see why young people, disillusioned and embittered by the experience of their own schooling and by what they have learned of the world around them, should want to drink hope and health at the fountain of childhood. But in that case, as I sometimes say to them, they should be paying the children they are "working with," not the other way around. On occasions I have asked some of these young people what they know or can do, what knowledge or skill they have to share, that would be so interesting and exciting to children that they would come to them of their own free will. Sometimes they have a good answer. Too often they have none. The young person who wants to "work with kids" is, like the most traditional school teacher, depending on society to deliver him a captive audience of kids to work with.

"The freedom to be a child" is a phrase much used. It sounds as if when a child is doing some things he is "being a child," while when doing others he is not. Better to say, according to the case, that at one moment or another a child is energetic, or gay, or sad, or angry, or absorbed, or vivacious, or bored, or frightened, or rebellious. But in all of these cases he remains a child. In my own growing up, some people and some experiences gave me pleasure, confidence, and strength, while others made me bored, anxious, afraid. Then as now, I wanted more of the good and less of the bad. But none of this connects for me in any way with words about "the freedom to be a child." In my childhood I was a child. What else could I have been?

"Allowed to experience childhood." At one level these words are true, but hardly worth saying. At any age, we experience being that age. Clearly the users of such words mean something else. Being allowed to experience childhood means being allowed to do some things and being spared having to do others—or *forbidden*. It means that adults will decide, without often or ever asking children what they think, that some experiences are good for children while others are not. It means for a child that adults are all the time deciding what is best for you and then letting or making you do it. But instead of trying to make sure that all children get only those experiences we think are good for them I would rather make available to children, as to everyone else, the widest possible range of experiences (except those that hurt others) and let them choose those they like best.

"Giving children time to grow." In one sense, the words mean nothing. How can one person *give* time to another? We can avoid taking or wasting someone's time, but that's not giving it. And the child is going to grow whether people give him time or not. If we want the child to grow not just in age, size, and strength, but in understanding, awareness, kindness, confidence, competence, and joy, then he needs not time as such but access to experiences that will build these other qualities. And he needs the right to shun and flee experiences that do the opposite, experiences all too common in the lives of most children—the experience of terror, of humiliation, of contempt, of endless anxiety, of deception, of lack of trust, of being denied choice, of being pushed around, of having his life filled with dull and pointless and repeated drudgery. But we all need this, so much that the lack of it is making us sick.

A child, we are often told, needs to feel that he is a human being in his own right. Yes, but which of us, of whatever age, does not need to feel this? Perhaps these words mean, at least in part, that children should not feel they are constantly being measured and judged against arbitrary standards. But that is the right of everyone. "Judge not, that ye be not judged." Those words mean that we may judge another man's act but not the man, that man is not knowable, measurable, that no one has the right to reduce the fullness and mystery of a human being, as our teachers, testers, and psychologists so often do, to a label or a group of numbers or a rank in a pecking order. We all have a right to feel that we are not just what other people, even experts, say we are—not just this race, or size, or color, or occupation, or income level, or position, or I.Q., or personality profile—but that there is an essence that is much larger, more unknowable, and more important. And it is a delusion to believe that even if this right is denied us it may somehow be given to children, that they may have a right to dignity and a unique and inviolable identity where no one else does.

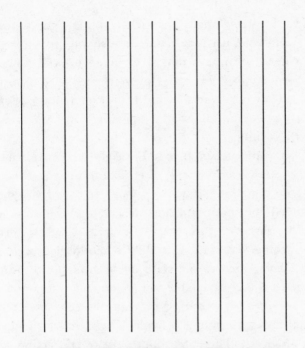

16. ON THE USE OF THE WORD "RIGHTS"

Much is said and written these days about children's "rights." Many use the word to mean something that we all agree it would be good for every child to have: "the right to a good home," or "the right to a good education." I mean what we mean when we speak of the rights of adults. I urge that the law grant and guarantee to the young the freedom that it now grants to adults to make certain kinds of choices, do certain kinds of things, and accept certain kinds of responsibilities. This means in turn that the law will take action *against* anyone who interferes with young people's rights to do such things. Thus when the law guarantees me the right to vote, it is not saying I must vote, it is not *giving* me a vote. It only says that if I choose to vote it will act against anyone who tries to prevent me. In granting me rights the law does not say what I must or shall do. It simply says that it will not allow other people to prevent me from doing these things.

This would not be true of the right to receive a guaranteed income. Here we speak of *requiring* the government or state to do something. To say that people have the right to a guaranteed minimum income means that the state is required by law to assure that all citizens have at least this much income. To grant this right to children would mean that whatever income the state made available to adults it must make equally available to the young.

There is no use telling the state to guarantee what it does not have and cannot provide. The state has money, and so can provide it. The state can promise to take action against people who in certain ways prevent a citizen, young or old, from choosing and acting. But the state cannot guarantee every child a good home and a good family. It does not have these things to give and cannot make or get them. What are its options if it tries to order everyone to make a good home for his child? In the first place, who decides, and on what grounds, whether the home is good? In one case reported in *Life* magazine the state took children away from their parents, whom they loved and wanted to stay with, because some psychologist had decreed the parents did not have a high enough I.Q. to raise a family—though they had been raising it. In other cases the state has taken unwilling children away from their parents because the neighbors and the community did not approve of the parents' lifestyle or politics. The state can decide things for very peculiar reasons. And if it has been decided, somehow, that the home is not good, what does the state do next? Take the child away? Has it other good homes to offer in place of this one? Suppose the child does not want to leave the home, bad as the state thinks it may be? Suppose he likes the old home better than the one the state has provided for him? Suppose he refuses to stay in the "good" home and keeps going back to the old home the state decided wasn't good enough? What happens now is that the state sends the police after him, to take him by force to the home of its choice. Or, if the state does not want to, or cannot, take the child away from a home that it considers bad, does it say to the parents, "This home is bad, make it good." And if they do not or cannot, what does the state do? Punish them? Will this make the home better?

What we can and should do is leave to the child the right to decide how good his home seems to be and give him the right if he does not like it to choose something else. The state may decide to provide or help provide some of these other choices. But it should not make these choices compulsory. It should allow the the child to make choices other than the ones it has provided. It should give the child the right to say no to *it* as well as to his parents.

One right I want for children is the right to work for money. Hearing this, people worry about protecting children against exploitation. I will say more about this later. A much harder task, as we have seen from the experience of women and minority groups, will be to protect the young against discrimination. In most places the law now says that employers in hiring and promoting may not discriminate against people on the grounds of race, sex, origin, and so forth. But it is very hard in practice to enforce this, to prove that when an employer hires or promotes this person over that, or fires this one rather than that, he is deciding on illegal grounds. Of course he will talk about "qualifications." Employers will find many reasons for not hiring the young. They may say, as some now do, often truthfully, that they cannot hire young people to work because their insurance does not cover them. If insurance companies are writing such clauses into their contracts, the law may have to take some action to prevent this.

In short, even if we win for the young the right to work, the hard problem will be to see that this right does not become a dead letter, a right in name only. This is one reason we are not likely to see such laws passed, much less made effective, in a society in which there is much poverty, unemployment, and discrimination.

As I will say many times, it is hard to say among these rights that this one is more important than that or that unless this one is granted that one cannot be. Some rights, to be effective, depend very much on the other rights being available; others are more able to stand alone. But even so, as we have found in the case of adults, these rights tend very much to go together. If all the rights I propose were available, many young people might not necessarily choose to use all of them at once, might only choose one or two. But they would probably not be able to use effectively the rights they wanted to use unless in a pinch they could use some of the others.

Take for example the right to leave home, to travel, to make one's own home. On the whole this right has no meaning unless the young person also has a right to earn money, to receive from the state a minimum income, and to be legally and financially responsible—to open a bank account, write checks, and so forth. But a young person in such a position will not be able to protect himself against cheating and exploitation (hard enough for adults right now) unless he can have the full use and protection of the law. This in turn is not likely to mean much unless he can vote. So perhaps the right to vote is most important and must come first. As a practical matter young people can probably get this right before they get others, and they will probably have to get it in order to get others. But even the right to vote can perhaps not be fully meaningful to a young person unless he can protect himself from undue pressure from his parents to vote the way they want. Elsewhere I suggest some ways in which society and the law might help him do this. But these can only be effective up to a point as long as the young person cannot get away from home and has no other place to go.

In the same way, the right of a young person to manage his own learning is a right that could and should be granted, and could be used, more or less independently of others. There is no reason why a child, living in every other way as a dependent of his parents, could not and should not have (like everyone else) the right to decide what he wants to learn, and when and how much of it he wants to learn in school, and in what school, and how much time he wants to spend doing it. But again, this right will not be fully effective unless he has some way of resisting or escaping whatever pressures his parents may put on him.

This is not to say that I think a society should or will pass an omnibus bill tying all these rights in one package. It seems likely that if the young gain these rights, they will only do so as a result of a long series of laws and court decisions, many of them affecting only one right at a time. But people working to gain these rights for the young will be wise to understand that no one of them, *by itself,* is likely to be very effective or to make a great deal of difference in the lives of the young people. If we care very much about some of them we will probably have to work for some of the others.

17. THE RIGHT TO VOTE

One of the most important rights that should be available to the young is the right to vote. This right does not need to and should not depend on a young person having or exercising other rights. In other words, a young person living in every other respect as a child, as a dependent, should have the same right as everyone else to vote, just as many adults living as dependents have it.

Though we will most probably lower the voting age a year or two at a time, ultimately, I want the right to vote for people of any age. No one should be left out.

The main reason why people should be able to elect their governments is not that they will necessarily choose better than a group of experts. It is first of all a matter of justice. If I am going to be affected by what you decide, I should have a say in it. If you are going to have control over me, then I should have some over you. Early Americans spoke of the injustice of taxation without representation, but there was, and is, more to it than taxation. To be in any way subject to the laws of a society without having any right or way to say what those laws should be is the most serious injustice. It invites misrule, corruption, and tyranny. That every so often the people in power have to make some kind of report to the voters, and get some kind of endorsement for what they have done or want to do, is obviously not much of a check on them. But it is better than no check at all.

The other great reason for giving people control over their government, and hence over their lives, is that it may and probably will make them more informed and responsible. People do not always learn from experience, but without it they do not learn at all. And experience alone is not enough; they must have not just experience but the ability to affect experience. If they think their choices and decisions make a difference to them, in their own lives, they will have every reason to try to choose and decide more wisely. But if what they think makes no difference, why bother to think? It is not just power, but impotence, that corrupts people. It gives them the mind and soul of slaves. It makes them indifferent, lazy, cynical, irresponsible, and, above all, stupid.

This has nothing to do with the sentimental belief that the average person or the mass of people have some mysterious wisdom or would never make any mistakes. They would make plenty. People are generally ignorant and fallible. But on the whole, most of the time, every human being knows better than anyone else what he needs and wants, what gives him pleasure and joy or causes suffering and pain. Given real choices, people will choose for themselves better than others will choose for them. What is much more important, every human being is likely to know better than anyone else when he has made a mistake, when a choice he has made is working badly. Given a chance to correct that mistake, he is more likely to do so than someone else.

A young man asked a wise man, a guru, what made a person wise. "Well," said the sage, "it is mostly a matter of good judgement." The young person asked how he could get good judgement. The sage replied, "By having the right kind of experience." The baffled young person cried out, "But how can I get that kind of experience?" The sage said, "By using bad judgement."

But some people will say, what about the people who are *always* making mistakes, who seem *never* to learn from them or even to want to learn from them? Why should the rest of us have to keep cleaning up their messes and paying for their mistakes? Why don't we just say, since you can't or don't want to keep yourself out of trouble, we are going to give you a keeper. One reply would be, with a keeper he *surely* never will learn. But the best answer is that in the long run the keepers wind up costing us more than the kept. Thus, if gambling were everywhere legal, a certain number of people would no doubt gamble their lives away. But the cost of supporting these compulsive gamblers in their habit would have been, and would still be, vastly less than the cost, in money and in the corruption of our governments and society, of our futile efforts to outlaw gambling. The Demon Rum never did this country anywhere near as much harm as Prohibition.

If democracy works as badly as it does, it is not so much because the people make mistakes, though they do, as because the people who run for office, their public servants, are so secretive and dishonest about what they do and mean to do. What happens too often is that people who crave political power decide privately what is best for the people and the country and then make whatever appeals and tell whatever lies they think will persuade people to give them that power. We might say of democracy or representative government what G. K. Chesterton once said of Christianity, not that it had been tried and found wanting but that it had been found difficult and not tried.

Furthermore, to deny the vote to the young is all the more unjust because they are likely to be more deeply affected than anyone else by the decisions the government makes and the things it does. A country may make a decision to go to war, or make a decision that will soon lead to war, in which young people will in a few years have to kill and die, but those young people will have nothing to say about the decision. A strong case could be made that on matters of war and peace no one should be able to vote who might not be called to fight. The matter of war aside, the young are more affected than anyone else by politics, because they will have to live longer with the consequences of what we do and any mistakes we make.

When I say that I want all young people to be able to vote, older people ask with amazement, disbelief, and even anger whether I mean children of any age. That is exactly

thing else. We have made a cult, a way of life, and (for adults) a profitable industry out of adolescence.

There is almost no evidence of what children themselves think about this. The magazine *Kids* printed a letter from me saying that I would like to know whether readers of the magazine felt that they should be allowed to vote and if they were allowed, whether they would. One teacher, Mrs. Paul, read my letter to her fourth-grade class at the Longfellow School in Holland, Michigan, and had them all write me letters telling how they felt. I don't know whether the children discussed my questions in class, or with their parents, before writing their letters. The children's replies fall into the following categories, with the indicated number of boys and girls voting in each category:

I would vote, and we should be allowed to	8B, 3G
I would vote	1B
I would vote, but children should not be allowed to	5B, 2G
I would not vote	1B (religious grounds)
We should not be allowed to	1G
I would not vote, and we should not be allowed to	4B, 4G

Those who said they would not vote, or that they should not be allowed to, gave these reasons (some gave more than one, some gave none):

161

Would not know how, not responsible, too difficult, etc.	10
Not fair to those who had to wait	4
Might break the voting machines	3
Would vote same way as parents	2

It is interesting that seven children should have said that they would vote if allowed but that children should not be allowed to. It reminds me a little of the children in my fifth-grade class, who in a certain setting would say hotly that any child who stole a pencil or pushed someone else at recess should be sent home or suspended from school for a week, though they regularly did those things themselves and would have been furiously (and rightly) indignant if such a severe punishment had been meted out to them. In this class, seven of those who said that children were for various reasons not smart enough to vote did not consider themselves to be one of such children. But much older children (and indeed often adults) say the same thing; any number of high school students have defended the strict rules in their school by saying that although they would behave without such rules most of the students would not.

On the other hand, when these fourth graders said that "children" should not be allowed to vote, they may not have meant themselves but children younger than themselves; perhaps they did not think of themselves as "children." Indeed, many fifth graders I have known were willing to think of themselves as kids, but not as "children."

Two of the children who said that they should not be allowed to vote because it would not be fair to the adults wrote as if they may not have understood the question. They may have thought I was asking if an exception to the law should be made in their case. But I am not sure of this.

Elsewhere I have described a meeting with ninth graders in which about two-thirds of them said that if they could vote, they would. But some of them may have been guessing what I wanted them to say or may have been trying to look "responsible" before the other adults in the room. A friend of mine, also in the ninth grade, asked a number of her friends and classmates whether they would vote if they could; according to her, most said they would not.

But what people say they will do if a situation arises and what they actually do in that situation are often very different. Most political experts believed that during the 1972 presidential campaign eighteen- to twenty-one-year-olds would register and vote in very large numbers and that in many states their votes would be decisive. This proved not to be the case. They registered and voted in about the same or slightly smaller percentages as older people, and they voted in about the same way. This failure to register and vote was a most serious and unwise political mistake. Young people explain and defend it by saying that they were disillusioned with both the candidates, the nominating process, and so forth. No doubt they had reason to be disillusioned, but their response was unwise none the less. Had they registered in force but voted very selectively or not at all, they would have made clear to the political leaders of both parties that there was a large bloc of voters out there who did not like what they were doing but were ready to support candidates they could trust. As things stand they have only convinced politicians that the youth vote is negligible and that anyone who makes any concessions to the needs or wishes of young people does so only at great political risk. Thus it is highly probable that being known as a youth candidate, though it did not get him many young people's votes, cost McGovern the votes of many older people. This sort of lesson will not be lost on candidates in future elections. They will see, as many do now, that it is much safer to be against the young than for them.

As a practical political matter, the voting age will probably not be lowered from eighteen to, say, sixteen until at least two things have happened. First, there must be a large bloc of sixteen- to eighteen-year-olds demanding the vote and saying to politicians, "If you deny us the vote now, we will remember you when we get it." And the politicians must know they mean it. Secondly, this bloc of sixteen- eighteen-year-olds must have made an alliance with some powerful groups of older voters, including, I would hope, most of the eighteen- to twenty-year-olds. I would like to say to those many young people who are now struggling to get students' " rights or to reform their schools—shoot at a target worth hitting. Forget students' rights and get yourselves the rights of citizens. Get the vote, and when you have it, get it for those younger than you are. The schools are not going to be reformed from within; their serious reform is a political matter and will be accomplished, if at all, with votes, not rallies and seizings of presidents' and deans' offices.

What I said earlier about the vote tending to make people more informed and responsible citizens is equally true of the young. The possibility of voting will stimulate an interest in voting. The possibility of exercising responsibility draws people toward it. Today, many young people might say, "Why should I interest myself in politics and voting, since no matter how much I know or learn, I can't vote."

Merely knowing they could vote if they wanted, or knowing people of their own age who voted, would do more to interest and inform the young about the society around them than anything, however "relevant," we could put in the curriculum or do in the school. It would be like an open door and a beckoning hand to the larger adult world. One question would lead to another. Why do people vote? What's the difference between those people they are voting for? What do those people do? (Questions, by the way, that few adults could answer.) Think of the excitement that is generated in a junior high or elementary school by nothing more than a school or class election, a Mickey Mouse affair in which nothing at all, except perhaps popularity, is at stake. Children talk about it and work on it for weeks. We often take this as proof that their concerns are childish— see how worked up they get about nothing. But we don't give them the chance to concern themselves with anything else.

A recent news photo showed a young child wearing a T-shirt marked "Snoopy For President." Such photos make us think, "Isn't that cute!" They also help us to feel sure that children do not really understand what the Presidency means and could not possibly think sensibly about it. What we forget is that it was not a child, but an adult, who had the bright idea of putting "Snoopy For President" on that T-shirt. Adults design such shirts, make them, buy them, and dress children in them. But the shirts tell us nothing of what children think or might think.

For some time I have been discussing these matters with "educated" audiences at colleges and universities. When I say that very young people should be allowed to vote, many of them react with fear and anger. At one meeting a man rose, voice shaking, and asked me what made me think—he could hardly get the words out—how could I imagine that a six-year-old child would know enough to know what to do about inflation. I said, "The President of the United States doesn't know what to do about inflation. Neither do the heads of state of any other countries that I know of. Or if they know, they can't or won't do it."

Most people assume that if young people voted they would vote foolishly, ignorantly, for trivial reasons. I don't think their reasons for voting would be any worse than those of many people who now vote, and often might be better. But even if it were certain that young people would vote more unwisely than most or all adults, this would not be a sufficient reason to deny them the vote.

There is much evidence that enormous numbers of people who now vote do so out of deep ignorance and for the most frivolous and foolish reasons. We have learned time after time that most people (in spite of their schooling) do not even *recognize* the Declaration of Independence or the Bill of Rights when they are typed out on ordinary paper and shown to them. When they are asked to sign these statements, the most fundamental documents of our society and supposedly the foundation of our political system, about nine out of ten people refuse, calling them radical, subversive, communist, which from the point of view of our present government I suppose they may well be. Two or three years after the start of the Korean War, the daily newspaper of a large city, one with a generally high level of education and culture, ran a current events poll on the sidewalks of the city, asking large numbers of passersby questions about what was going on in the world. One question was, "Where, roughly, is Korea?" For the purposes of their poll, such answers as, "On the Pacific Ocean," "Near Japan," "Near

China," and so on, would have been judged correct. But more than half of the people asked could not give even that good an answer. More recently, in the presidential campaign of 1972, we had the infamous Watergate scandal, which as I write this (April 1973) is slowly forcing its way to the attention of the American public. But well into the campaign in the fall of 1972, when the Watergate affair had over and over again been in the papers and magazines and on TV, only a third of the people in one national poll could even identify the name and only half of those had any idea of what it meant. And this is one of the most significant and sinister events of American politics in the whole history of the country.

Not long ago there was a very hotly fought congressional election in the district that included part or all of Palo Alto, California. Thee Republican incumbent had been in the House a long time and supported the Indo-China war; the Democratic challenger, a minister, opposed it. Palo Alto being a rich community, as well as the home of Stanford University, a great deal of money and work went into the campaign. Leaflets and notices were everywhere, and door-to-door canvassers talked with large numbers of voters. Probably not in one campaign out of a hundred do the candidates and the issues get such exposure. After the election, which the Republican won, some sociologists decided to find out why voters voted as they did—what they thought of the issues, what issues they thought were important, what kinds of appeals and methods of canvassing were effective and what were not. They found that an overwhelming majority of those voters to whom they talked—a quite carefully chosen sample—knew *almost nothing* about the issues of the campaign. They had voted as they did because they liked the man's face, or his name, or because he seemed older and more experienced, or because they thought a change might be good, or because they had always voted Democratic or Republican and saw no reason to change. A considerable percentage of voters even got mixed up about which candidate was for what issues or belonged to which party. That is, there were pro-war people who voted for the anti-war candidate, and vice-versa, and there were people who thought they had voted for the Republican (or the Democrat) who did not know, until the interviewer talked to them, that they had in fact voted for the opposite party. The lack of information and the amount of misinformation among these voters—and this in a supposedly highly educated community and after an intensely waged campaign—was hardly believable.

No amount of ignorance, misinformation, or outright delusion will bar an adult from voting. There are still people in the country who believe that the earth is flat, or hollow; yet they can vote. Many still believe in a literal interpretation of the Bible, that the world was created in seven days or that Woman was created from Man's rib, and so on; yet they can vote. Henry Ford, the founder of the Ford Motor Company, was (for much of his life) one of a number of people who believed in a mythical document called the Protocols of the Elders of Zion, which purports to be the record of a conspiracy of Jews to take over the world. Yet he could vote. There are people who thought that Asia was made of dominoes. There are people who think that all other people are machines. There are, in short, people who believe all manner of absurd, fantastic, and even dangerous things. None of them are barred from voting. Why should young people be? There is no reason to believe that the reasons for which most adults vote are better than the reasons for which young people would vote if they could. Politicians, office-seekers, understand this well. It has been a fundamental principle of American politics for many years, frequently written about, and terrifyingly supported by the 1972 presidential elections, that the surest way to be elected is to stay as far as possible away from the issues and concentrate instead on projecting an Image.

Some ask, "Isn't there a danger that if children could vote their parents would simply tell them whom to vote for and threaten to punish them if they did not." Perhaps. But a society which had changed enough in its way of looking at young children to be willing to grant them the vote would be one in which few people would want or try to coerce a child's vote and in which most people would feel this was a very bad and wrong thing to do. In such a society, whoever tried to coerce a child's vote would feel a heavy weight of public disapproval, which very few people like or can stand against. And the child himself would feel strongly supported in defying the attempt of his parents, or anyone else, to coerce him. Loving and respectful parents would trust instead in whatever natural influence they might have over him. Even if he voted the opposite way from them, they might well value his courage and independence. On the other hand, if relationships in the family were bad, and the parents did not love or respect the child, then he would be all the more ready to defy them. We should remember, too, that many people today vote at first, and often for many years after, exactly as their parents voted. We are all deeply influenced, in politics as everything else, by the words and example of people we love and trust. Children's votes would of course be influenced by their parents. Intelligent and respectful parents, with the natural authority of talent, kindness, and wisdom, would probably have the most influence. Why should not the influence of such people be multiplied through the votes of their children? Some ask if this might not give a disproportionate influence to those (usually poor) people in society who had the most children. This possibility, if it exists at all, is certainly no reason for denying young people the vote.

Some have agreed that the principle of allowing younger people to vote seemed right and just, but that there should be some requirements, that they should have to pass some sort of a test. On the face of it, it seems reasonable enough. If someone could persuade me that we had a sure way to measure a person's wisdom and judgment, as we might put a thermometer in his mouth to take a temperature, I would at least entertain the argument that no one, of any age, should be able to vote unless his wisdom rating was above a certain level. But such arguments are purely theoretical. No such test or measure of wisdom exists, or in the nature of things can exist, and even if it did, there is no way to be sure that such a test would be given and used honestly. From our too recent history we know how the literacy requirement in many Southern states was used to bar from voting black men and women whose learning and judgement were fifty times that of the white people barring them—black lawyers and university graduates would be declared ineligible by white people who could barely write their names. And even in this last election we had case after case, all over the country, in which local election authorities, in clear defiance of the law, tried by various means to deny to young people the vote that the law and the courts had given them. There is simply no way in which we could devise a proper test for voters or insure that it would be used fairly and not to the benefit of whoever happened to control the election machinery. The only answer is to give the vote to everyone who wants it, do all we can to see that they have access to information that will help them vote wisely, and hope for the best.

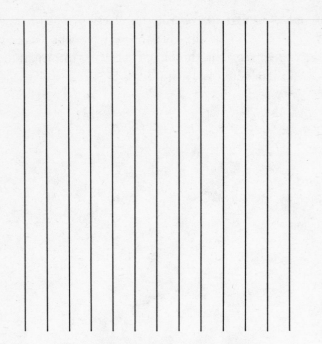

18. THE RIGHT TO WORK

Children, of any age, should have the right to work for money and to own and use, spend or save, the money they earn. This right, like the right to vote or to manage one's own learning, can stand alone. It could be granted to young people even if no other adults rights were granted.

Today child labor laws deny this right to the young. As in the case of the vote, if the working age limit is lowered, it will probably be only a year or two at a time. For reasons I have pointed out, it will probably not be lowered at all except in societies that by political and economic means have ended severe poverty and unemployment. As with other rights, young people of any given age will not get the right to work until considerable numbers of them, voting themselves or with allies, demand that right. Nor will this right be granted until many older people think of the young of that age as intelligent, capable, and serious people that they would want to have working with or for them. Attitudes will have to change before we can change the law.

There are many reasons why many children would like to work and why it would be good for them to be able to. They need or want the money they could earn to buy things they like, to save up for the future. Perhaps most important, in a consumer society like ours to be without money makes most people feel left out, a non-person; to have one's own money, even when not a matter of need, is a matter of self-respect. Children of rich parents can earn money now in many ways. It is the children of the poor who have no legitimate and honorable way to get money. This is certainly an important reason why more of them, and at younger ages, are turning to crime—stealing, picking pockets, snatching purses, mugging, and the like. Some may do it for adventure, a test of skill and nerve, or to impress their peers. Still others may do it out of spite and malice, making up for the emptiness and pain of their own lives with the pleasure of terrifying and dominating others. Perhaps some such people would rather steal than work and would continue to steal even if they could work. But I think that most poor youngsters who now steal would much rather earn money legitimately if they could.

During the 1950s young people in many large cities formed gangs, each defending a turf and fighting other gangs. Gang activity grew less during the late 60s, but it has now flared up again and in many cities is an increasingly serious and even terrifying problem. Today's gangs are bigger, armed with real guns instead of homemade weapons, and are increasingly criminal and violent. No one seems to have the least idea what to do about them. We might for a start try letting them grow up. Many of those who wrote about gangs and gang members in the 1950s asked the question: What (other than being killed or jailed) makes gang members give up the gang life? In most cases the answer was, being able to get a job, to have money, to get away from their families, to make their own homes, and to get married and start their own families. What was even more striking was that when a gang member became old enough to do these things, the younger gang members did not try to keep him in the gang but let him go, as if they knew very well that gang life was kid stuff, to be given up when you had a chance to do something more grown-up and serious.

Work is novel, adventurous, another way of exploring the world. Many defend the boredom and drudgery of the schoolroom by saying that we have to teach children what work is like. Why make the schoolroom dull in order to do that, when most children *want to find out* what work is like and for a while at least would not find it dull at all? Many children, often the most troublesome and unmanageable, want to be useful, to feel that they make a difference. Real work is a way to do this. Also, work is a part of the mysterious and attractive world of adults, who work much of the time. When a child gets a chance to work with them, he sees a new side of them and feels a part of their world. He also sees a glimpse of his own future. Someday he too will be big and will work most of the time; now he can find out what it will be like.

A young person I once knew, not happy in his quite pleasant and kindly school, was eager to get a job. He wanted to find out what work was like. His friends were doing it, he could make much more money this way than he got in his allowance, and it would be his money in a way that the other was not. But though he never said as much, I suspect he wanted to work partly to be in a different relationship with adults. The only relationship he knew had been an irresponsible and dependent one. The adults had been caring for him and worrying about him. Some of these adults he liked, others he did not, but he could not resist or escape their claim that he had to do what they told him because it was all for his good. Working in a store, he would never hear that. He might be ruled by the wishes and orders of the customers and his boss, but he would be doing something *for them*, a real service however small. Also, he would be putting his energy and skill into a real activity. The store existed not to help him but to sell stuff, provide a service, earn money. He would be judged, when he was, against these concrete and sensible aims. He might hear, "How many times do I have to tell you that these go with these?" Or, "Hurry up and get that back room cleaned up." Or praise and thanks, if it was earned. Nothing as vague as the reasons for which he was constantly judged at school: he was disappointing people, his attitude was poor, he would not get into college, he would not be a success. In a store there would usually be an immediate and clear connection between what he was asked or told to do and the work and health of the store. How different from school, full of what Peter Marin called "artificial rituals of act and consequence," where good or bad is whatever the teachers say is good or bad, where there is no clear reason for doing anything except that someone tells you to do it.

Work often makes a visible difference in the world. The fortunate and rare child who can help some adults make or build something will be able for many years to look at what they did and think, "I helped do that." Work often demands and tests much of a child's strength and skill. He often is able to use interesting machines and tools that otherwise, in school or out, he would never be able to touch. What could be more exciting, for a child just old enough to do it, than to run a vacuum cleaner or a mixing machine or a power lawn-mower or a tractor. What toys could compare with them? An eight- or nine-year-old I knew would not let anyone else in his family mow the lawn with the power mower. It was very hard for him to push it, but it was his tool and his work. Later some of this novelty and excitement wore off, and mow-ing the lawn became one of those things that every so often just had to be done. But for a while that work was one of the high points of his life.

Many say, with A. S. Neill of Summerhill, that children don't like to work, won't work unless forced to, and would rather play. Many parents, who have tried for years to get their children to help them with chores around the house, would agree. There are certainly some kinds of work that children don't like and won't do unless pushed hard. But many of these tasks are things, like housework, that no one likes to do. On the recording "Free to Be You and Me" produced by *MS* magazine, Carol Channing sings a very funny song about housework and the women we see doing it on TV. They are always smiling, she points out, and the reason is not that they like housework but that they are actresses and are getting paid to *pretend* to do housework.

But nobody does real housework with a smile. It is no fun, so everyone in a family—men, women, boys, girls—should do a share of it.

When we talk about children and work, one difficulty we have is saying what we mean by work and how it differs from play. Some say that work is what has a serious purpose, play is what does not. But who decides what is serious? The worker or the watcher? Some people play games, or music, for money; others do not. Are those who play for money necessarily more serious? I am just as serious playing tennis, or playing the cello, as I am doing things I get paid for. Perhaps someone who had to do really dull or unpleasant or dangerous work would say that people who write or make music for a living don't know "what real work is." Certainly some of the things that people call work are much more interesting, exciting, and pleasant than others. To a large extent, the kinds of work that children don't like to do, no one likes to do.

Neill makes this distinction between work and play— that children can fantasize about play but not about work and that since their fantasy lives are important to them this is why they like to play and not work. There is certainly some truth is this; it would be hard to fantasize about washing dishes. On the other hand, when I write a book, I do quite a bit of fantasizing about it, imagine it being well-reviewed, being read, making a difference in people's lives. Indeed, when I can't imagine the book finished, existing, and doing well, I can't write it. It isn't real for me. It seems a waste of time banging out words that no one will ever read or pay any attention to. In any case, those are mistaken who say contemptuously that children are lazy and will only do what is easy unless forced to do what is hard. When I first saw

Summerhill, many of the children, even very young ones, had dug enormous holes and caves in the ground. Certainly they had a serious purpose in doing this and certainly the work took a great deal of energy and skill, and commitment as well—many of those caves must have taken weeks to dig and indeed none of them ever seemed to be what we would call finished.

Fantasy is important. Children like to do things and make things that free and engage their imaginations, that they can use in their fantasies and daydreams. But, as a few countries seem to be learning in their experience with playgrounds, and as we in the U.S. seem to be slow to learn, children resist having their fantasizing done for them. Adults think that if they build something that looks like, say, a whale, children will play all kinds of games with it and on it in which they imagine themselves doing something with a real whale. Not so; what most children try to do with such ready-made whales is try to find out how to take them apart. Their purpose is indeed serious; and since the whale is usually made of tough plastic or concrete, reinforced with steel, and since the children have primitive tools, the work is very hard. But they almost always get the job done; such ready-made playgrounds have short lives. On adventure or construction playgrounds children are constantly building things, sawing, hammering, nailing, using with great energy and persistence tools which are often too big for them, unfamiliar, and difficult. What is important is that they are in charge of the work. They are building something they want to build and deciding how they will do it. In that respect, clumsy as they may be, they are craftsmen rather than laborers. Also important is that they do have a fantasy purpose in building what they are building—it is going to be a ship, or a tower, or a hotel, or a secret club. All kinds of exciting things are going to happen in and on it, are already happening in their minds. But fantasy works better when it has something real to work with, as Ben Rogers, driving his imaginary steamboat down the street, found out when he met Tom Sawyer wielding a real whitewash brush.

There are other reasons why children don't like to do many of the small jobs and chores we often ask them to do. One is that they often have to do these tasks alone. Young children I have known, who hated to clean up their rooms, didn't mind it when I or someone else did it with them. We found many ways to make a game or contest of it, they pitched in and worked hard, and the job was soon done. Many of the house chores that children now resist they would be more glad to do if they could do them with someone else.

Another reason why children don't like many of the tasks we ask or tell them to do is that they don't see the need, the end we have in mind. When we take the garbage out, we know the reason: if we don't take it out the kitchen will eventually be full of garbage. In our mind's eye we can see it there, we can almost smell it. In this sense we could be said to have a *more* active fantasy life than the children. The child has no such fantasy. We may ask him, "What do you think would happen if we didn't take out the garbage?" He has no idea. He thinks, I suppose, the sack of garbage would just sit there where it is, what's so bad about that. Alfred Korzybski, the general semanticist, who wrote *Science and Sanity,* called human beings time-binders, and one difference between older and younger people is that (in many respects) the older can bind more time, can see better how what we did then led to what we do now and how what we do or don't do now may lead to something else—perhaps a house full of garbage, perhaps a yard with grass three feet high. Or we do other things that to a child might seem a waste of time because we see a good end in mind. We plant a tiny tree seeing in our fantasy the big tree it will become, how beautiful it will be, how much shade and pleasure it will give us. How could a child imagine this? He might be glad to join us in planting a tree because when it was in the ground he could look at it and think that he helped put it there. To be able to imagine it as a big tree—that takes time.

Much of the work we want a child to do seems endless, never finished. He is right, it *is* never finished. It will have to be done over and over again. Sometimes he thinks, what's the point of this. Why make my bed when I am just going to have to mess it up again tonight when I get in it? Not a bad question—I don't know the answer to it myself. In someone else's house I usually make my bed because I know that if I don't someone else will and why should they have to—but I don't really see why it needs to be made up. All that tucking in and smoothing down. What's the point? To make it look as if it had never been slept in—when someone sleeps in it every night?

Some of the work we do and try to make children do with us has purposes for us that it cannot have for them. My father loved gardening; we always had a vegetable garden. His father had grown up on a farm which the family had lived on for many generations and which his brother still farmed, so there was a family tie to the land. This is not something a child would know or understand or feel the weight of. Also gardening was in many ways the opposite from and therefore a balance to his life in the city, which he did not like, and to the work he did there, which was abstract —like many people he was in a business in which he did not make a product that he could see and feel. Vegetables were real; you put the seed in the ground and do various things and after a while there is something that you can pick and eat. None of this is important to a child. Nothing in the world is abstract to him, everything is equally concrete and tangible; a vegetable is as much but no more a miracle than anything else. So this work in the garden, which had many kinds of meaning to my father, seemed to us children endless, never-finished work to no purpose. Small wonder we resisted it as best we could. And the same could probably be said of the children at Summerhill, who did not want to help Neill with his garden and did not know why he got so upset when they swiped his tools.

In this talk about gardens and growing things I have touched on a more general purpose of adults' work, which children do not and cannot share with us. The child accepts the world as it is. He has more than enough work to do to explore it, find out about it, learn how to live in it. He is always pleased when he can change it, make some visible mark on it, and if he has no other way to do this he will write (often interesting) grafitti on walls or tear apart concrete and steel playgrounds. But there is no great hurry about this; life without end seems to stretch ahead of him. As we get older, though, time goes faster, life becomes more finite and short, we sense how very small and temporary we are against the immensity of time and space or even against the whole life of mankind; and with an urgency that young people cannot be expected to share, we want to change the world, if only in a very small way, to leave, like Kilroy, a mark to show that we were here.

At least by implication I have said something about the kinds of work that children like to do. Let me add a bit more to this. Children like work in which they can get their hands on, or better *in*, the materials. Hence part of the charm of the mud pie. They like to mix things, to feel textures, see colors. They like to feel these things changing. They love to control and use water; watering things out of a hose was always pleasant. Digging ponds or ditches, diverting or damming up water, all this is good work.

Many children, particularly if they are young enough, love to cook. In any elementary school or class in which cooking is a possible activity, it is always a favorite. All the stuff you use, perhaps with the exception of yukky eggs (which soon get transformed into something else), looks so good, smells so good, feels so good. There is quite a bit of change and magic in it; things start out looking one way and soon look like something else. There is suspense; will the cookies, cake, or whatever come out right? The child knows he will not have long to wait to find out; the end product will come soon. And when that product appears, the child knows he can use it, knows how to use it, and likes to use it. From the beginning his purpose and vision are clear, his time-binding firm. He thinks, I am going to make brownies and then I am going to *eat* them.

Painting is also good work. The tool is docile and sensuous; nothing could be more satisfying than the motion of the bristles of a paint brush against the wall. The paint itself has a lovely thick texture and a definite color. And what is important in all work for children, you can see as you work how the task is going and how much is left to do. Every new stroke of the brush brings a new sense of accomplishment. The brush also lends itself to fantasy; whenever I paint something, which is not often, it is not too long before I am telling myself that I am painting it extremely well.

If the tools are unfamiliar, exotic, and to a certain degree dangerous, and above all if they involve fire and heat, children like them all the more. At the Nye Lilleskole (New Little School) in Bagsvaerd, outside of Copenhagen, the children, the oldest of whom are fourteen, do welding. Anybody who wants to do it is allowed to do it. Some of the most ardent and skilled welders are under ten, and at least one of them has become as skillful as the adult who showed him how. It is one of the most popular activities in the school. It is hard to imagine welding equipment in most American elementary school classrooms, and indeed as long as schools are compulsory and therefore subject to all kinds of lawsuits if children get hurt, it is easy to understand their not allowing welding. But to my knowledge no one has yet been hurt welding at the Nye Lilleskole. And even if all schools did it, welding would probably cause fewer injuries than football.

Any work is good for children in which they can see what they are doing, how much they are doing, and how well they are doing it. Running a vacuum cleaner may be fun for a while, but once you get used to the machine, not much happens. Occasionally the vacuum cleaner sucks up a bit of paper or string, which is nice to see. Most of the time you can hardly tell where you have vacuumed or whether your work has made any difference. In my father's garden, weeding was one of the worst of chores. It seemed endless, and since we did not share his fantasy of the garden disappearing under giant weeds, it seemed pointless. But there was one job I loved. Now and then a section of grass had to be turned over and prepared for planting, or a part of the garden had to have fertilizer dug into it and turned over. This work took real effort. I could see why it had to be done. And I could see as I worked how I was doing. Every spadeful left its mark.

Now I could say, I'm one-quarter through; later, half-way through; later, three-quarters through; and finally the undug part would get smaller and smaller and—triumph!—finally disappear. This is part of what later made mowing a lawn, or cutting hay in a field, fun for me; I could compare the part mowed or cut with the part still left to do; one part grows, the other shrinks, and each part changes shape, until the finished has eaten up the unfinished. Children like this. Sawing a log or a piece of wood has this same feature. The work is hard, the saw may move very slowly, the worker may often have to rest his aching arm. But as he works he sees the groove cut by the saw eat deeper and deeper into the wood, and even if it seems to be going very slowly, the grains of sawdust coming out tell that something is happening.

If it has a purpose he can understand, if it takes his strength and skill, and if he can see the results of his work as he works, a child will undertake and stick at very hard tasks. What is important is not to give a child a job so big that it looks infinite, so big that he cannot measure or imagine any progress, so big that no matter how hard he works he seems to be standing still. Too big a task is like too much food on the plate; it defeats both imagination and appetite. He cannot imagine ever getting to the end of that task or plateful, so why even bother to start? Early in the work of writing a book I am often overcome and blocked by such feelings and have to think of tricks to keep myself going until in my fantasy the book begins to take shape and become real.

We may often wait too long before asking children to help us or letting them help when they ask. They may begin to ask at an age when we don't think of them as being able to be very helpful. Perhaps they want to vacuum the rug. But we know that they won't have much system and will probably miss many places so that we will have to do it again, and we think, it's too much trouble, easier to do it myself. But it might be wiser to let children try to help us even when they are too young to help very much. We should not assume that because they are clumsy they are not serious about helping. When he was three and a half, a boy I know saw his mother set the table and wanted to help her. She was having company and was using her favorite plates, and the floor was hard enough so that any dropped plate would break, so she said no. But the child insisted, so finally she showed him how to hold the plate very carefully with both hands, walk so that he could see where he was going, and put the plate carefully on the table. Neither then nor since has he ever dropped a plate, and in many ways he has been helpful ever since. Of course it is not always as easy as this; children are not all equally helpful, and even those who are most willing may not want to help when we need it most or in the way we need it most.

Still, I think we must honor and encourage in children their desire to be helpful and useful when it first appears. If we do not, they may lose it. We may leave them with the feeling that we don't trust them and that they are incapable of being helpful or useful. Or, perhaps, that we don't really need their help—otherwise why didn't we accept it when they first offered it. Or they may feel that the work we want them to do doesn't really need doing and that it is just something adults do to keep themselves occupied.

Most of what I have just written about children helping adults has obviously been about the middle-class family. Poor children, often from large families, are used to helping quite early in their lives. They may be asked to run errands, to go out to get food or medicine while their parents are busy or minding smaller children, or they may often mind smaller children themselves. In Mexico, and (I would guess) in many American cities, it is not uncommon to see children younger than three or even two being looked out for by children no older than six. Is this a bad thing? It may be if the older child has to do it all the time, as may sometimes be the case; he should have some time of his own. But quite a bit of this caring for younger children would probably do a child no harm and might do much good. From everything I could see the little children who were watching out for smaller ones seemed to be affectionate, interesting, and responsible companions, and lively and energetic in their own right.

"But," say some people, "if children could choose to work for money, this would only bring back the terrible days of child labor." There are many reasons why this is unlikely, and there are many things we can do, without taking from children their right to work, to prevent it.

What made the child labor of the nineteenth century so horrible was, in the first place, that children did not choose and could not refuse to do it. They were almost literally slaves, pressed into labor by their parents, themselves so dreadfully poor that without the little money brought in by the labor of the child they could not have kept the family alive. Half-starved already, had the child not worked, he would have starved altogether. But if he was a slave he was no more so than his parents, and, like them, he had no choice about what work he could do. He could not shop around, bargain, wait for something to turn up. He had to take what was offered when it was offered.

Poverty made that child a slave, and it was not so much child labor laws as it was the lessening of poverty that freed him. There are not a great many children in our society—

though even one would be too many and a disgrace to us all —who are as poor as most of the child workers of the nineteenth century. But any that there are, and in spite of whatever the law may say, work right now as much as they can. They need the money, and any money they can earn does them more good and meets their immediate and deepest needs far more than anything they could do, or anyone could do for them, if they were not working. They don't get the right food or enough of it as it is, and if they can't get money by working they will be getting even less. In both the short and the long run this is much worse for them than, say, missing school, and would be even if they were learning a lot in school and were being helped there. In short, to the extent that child labor laws keep our poorest children from working, they do them no great favor.

The next thing that made child labor terrible was the work itself. It was too hard, too demanding, too much for the child's strength. It went on too long; fourteen and even sixteen hours days were not uncommon. And it was done too often in terribly unhealthy and dangerous conditions. But all of this was as true for adults as for the child. The mines and the mills and the sweatshops were no less horrible for them. They too were mangled in machinery, poisoned by dust and chemicals, killed in accidents, drained of their health and strength. Women sewing in the garment shops of New York often lost their sight. One particularly dreadful statistic comes back to me. The economist and industrial consultant Peter Drucker once wrote that the average working life of the migrant laborers who built our great railroads was *five years*. This compares very well with the destructiveness of Stalin's slave labor camps, about which we have been so indignant. Our modern economy, of which we are so proud, like the economy of most great industrial nations, was built no less than Russia's on human bones and blood.

Finally, children were exploited because, like their parents, they were grossly underpaid for their work and because, since it was needed for the family, they could not keep or use any of the money they earned.

But though we have far more and worse poverty than a rich nation should, we do not have much of the poverty common in the nineteenth-century industrial towns. And, as I have pointed out, we are not likely to give children the right to work unless and until we find ways to have much less poverty than we do now. In such a society, in which none would fear the desperate poverty that created child labor, no one would be compelled to work long hours at degrading, destructive, and dangerous work or to try to force children into it. Indeed, even today, few people, except perhaps for some miners and low-paid agricultural field workers, work under conditions as bad as those common in the last century. There simply is not much of that kind of work for *anyone* to do, adults or children, and, hence, little reason to believe that children will be forced to do it.

There remains, of course, the possibility that for reasons not of fear and want but of envy and greed, the desire to keep up a certain "standard of living," people may still try to compel their children to work to earn money for the general family budget. In many families the husband holds two jobs, and the wife may work as well, so that they can afford at least some of what is waved in front of their noses every day on the TV. Or perhaps, so that they can buy their children the schooling they hope will lift them to a higher place in society. Might they not, if they could, tell the children that they too had to pitch in? It is possible. In most cases, I don't think it is likely. Again, we must think about a society in which large numbers of people feel very differently than they do now about the rights and dignity of the young. It is also possible that some children might want to work to earn money for their own purposes but that their parents would demand that any money they earned be put in the general family budget. All of these questions lead to a larger one: how do we protect certain of the rights of children, defend them, or enable them to defend themselves, against certain kinds of parent pressure and coercion, in a situation in which the children cannot yet or do not want to live away from home?

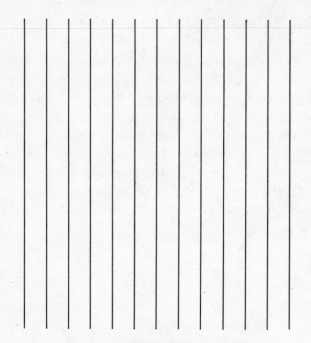

19. THE RIGHT TO OWN PROPERTY

Children should have the right to own at least some property. This is altogether apart from the much larger right to full financial independence and responsibility, which I also want for them, including the right to buy and sell property, borrow money, make contracts, and do everything financially that an adult may legally do. But this latter right may be a long time in coming. Meanwhile the law might first grant to children, otherwise living as dependents, the right to own property. And even if both the smaller and larger right were available, many children might want to claim only the smaller.

Today, as far as I know, a child, what the law calls a minor, has no right to own anything. Nothing he has belongs only and finally to him. It belongs to his parents or guardians and is his only if, and as long as, they choose to let him have it. The clothes on his back belong to his parents, who have the right to take them and dispose of them—though they are also obliged by law to keep him clothed. Even the money he earns by himself, by his own work, does not belong to him. Property can be set aside and held for him until he comes of legal age. But he cannot own anything in the here and now.

Today, many moderate- or high-income families act much of the time as if what was once given to the child, or bought by him with money he earned or saved or received as gifts, is his and cannot be taken away. But even this is true only within limits. Most children cannot spend more than fairly trivial amounts of money, earned or not, without their parents' permission. And there is a general understanding that the parents, whether for reasons of safety, or punishment, or whatever, have the right at any time to take away from a child, for as long as they choose, anything they don't want him to have.

When the child asks, "Can I have a so-and-so?" the parents may reply, "No, you're too young for it, you don't need it, we have no place to put it, they're too dangerous, they're no good, you'll soon get tired of it, they're a waste of money, you just want it because everyone else has it." Sometimes these objections may be sound. Sound or not, these decisions or whims of the parent are final. The child's right to own property is only the right to own whatever property they think he should own.

This in general does not seem to me wise or fair. But there may be a conflict between the right of a child to own what property he wants and the right of a parent or guardian, who cannot kick the child out, to determine what should be in his house. Thus, if a child living in cramped quarters, or in apartments near neighbors, wanted to have a set of drums or something equally noisy, a parent ought to have the right to say no to that, either because he can't stand the noise or because the noise will cause a lot of trouble with the neighbors or landlord, which the child won't be responsible for and won't have to deal with. It is only fair that whoever owns or rents a dwelling or is held responsible for what happens in it can decide what happens. This need not be a harsh rule if the young people in the house have other options, can go to other places to do what they want to do. In a humane society, there would be such places and options.

I propose that we write into law the principle that what is given to a child by his parents, relatives, or friends, or what he earns with his own work, is his, to keep or use as he wants, subject (as with any adult, but no more than with any adult) to the rules of his house, the concern of his neighbors, and the laws of the community. For example, no one of any age should be able to drive a motorcycle or car up and down a street at night (or any other time) with the muffler cut out. But people who would not be able to forbid an adult to do something, or would not be backed by the law if they did, ought not to have the right to forbid it to a child.

This raises some questions. How do we decided what is a child's property? If he earns money, that is obviously his. If he gets a gift from someone, that is his. But what about the furnishings in his room? Could he sell them or replace them? I would say no, not unless his parents agreed. What about his clothes? It costs a lot of money to keep a growing child in clothes. Once a child gets a garment of some kind, is it permanently his, to sell if he feels like it or has no more use for it? Again, certainly in families with little money, I would think not. The clothes are supplied for his use, like the furniture in his room, and they are his against the claim of anyone else in the family, other brothers and sisters, for instance. He should not have the right to sell anything his parents would have both a moral and legal obligation to replace. Furthermore, when he outgrew clothes or no longer wished to wear them, the parents should have, as now, the right to use them for a younger child or to trade them with the parents of other children or to use them in some other way. The same would go for supplies bought for school or perhaps certain kinds of athletic equipment. Things that parents must and do supply in order for the child to lead his life ought in the long run to belong to them, to dispose of as they see fit when he no longer can or wants to use them.

Thus, if a family spent scarce money to buy a child a bike so that he could ride to school or ride with his friends or perhaps sell papers or do some other kind of work, it would not be right for the child to sell that bike so that he could use the money for something else.

Toys are a difficult borderline case. They are more personal, and a child who gets attached to a particular object ought to have the right to keep it, even if the parents think he is too old for it or that a younger child ought to have it. A boy I know, going on eleven as I write this, has a large collection of stuffed koala bears of all sizes. This has been his favorite animal since he was very small, indeed almost the only kind of animal-doll toy he has ever been interested in. These bears are important to him; he knows them all, keeps track of them, and likes to sleep with quite a large number of them. Not very long ago his mother asked if he expected to have somewhat fewer of these bears around him when he grew up, left home, and lived in a place of his own. He said firmly, "I expect to have more!" He should have the right to keep his bears as long as he wants.

Let us say, and put into law, that what a child earns or buys with money earned or given to him or what is given to him as a gift is his property, to use and/or dispose of as he sees fit.

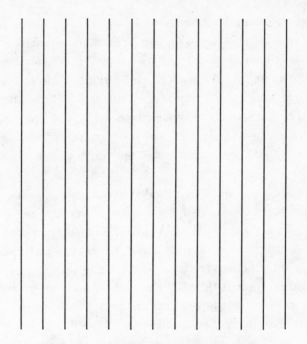

20. THE RIGHT TO TRAVEL

Young people should have the right to travel and to live away from home without parents' permission. Unlike some rights, this one cannot very well stand alone. Without the right to own, earn, or otherwise receive money, most young people haven't the means to travel very far from home or to stay away very long. Also, if young people do not have the right to be financially and legally responsible for themselves, someone else must be, and we cannot fairly hold such persons responsible for the acts of a young person they cannot see or control. Elsewhere I discuss these other rights. Here I would like to discuss the right to travel itself.

Most young people like to travel. They like adventure, and for most people travel is one of the few kinds of adventure left. It is a good way to find out many things about the world that can't be put down in books. And simply learning to live and get around in a strange community where one does not speak the language can test our ingenuity and intelligence.

Young people would travel more and sooner if they were allowed to. Many do in spite of difficulties and the law itself. In most states hitchhiking is illegal. Some states enforce this very strictly, even make it illegal to pick up hitchhikers and fine drivers who do so. None the less the young still do it, though they tend to tell each other to shy away from states where the laws are strictest. Much is made of the danger that hitchhikers, particularly female, may be attacked and killed. Now and then it happens. But deaths due to hitchhiking are very rare compared with deaths in ordinary auto accidents. An important reason for anti-hitchhiking laws, particularly in states where tourism is a big business, is not so much to prevent people from being injured or killed as to keep people without much money, "bums" and "hippies," out of the state.

Hitchhiking is, or was, a very popular way for young people to travel in Europe. Because of traditional attitudes of men toward women in Southern European countries, it may still not be a good idea for young women to hitchhike there, even with other women. But in Northern Europe even single girls can hitchhike safely. Everyone understands that it is good for young people to move about and see other places while they can and that they can't do it if it costs much money. Of course, as tourism becomes big business, as people get more and more money from travelers and therefore don't want poor ones, European countries may begin to make it harder for the young to travel. But in this they are far behind us.

Some of the prejudice against the traveling young comes from the fear that they use drugs. Some has to do with the fact that the young look peculiar. Much is simply the prejudice of a money-spending, buy-now-pay-later society against people who don't need, want, own, or buy a lot of stuff. One ski town has been for many summers a base from which many young people make backpacking trips into the mountain high country. Many of these young are not really poor; they are college students, and they often own good bikes and camping equipment. But a ten-speed bike doesn't support the local gas stations, and backpacking equipment, even the best, means that most of the time the owner will be sleeping in a tent somewhere and not in a twenty-five-dollar-a-day motel. So the merchants and businessmen complain about the young people ruining the town, and being bad for business, and keeping the spending tourists away, and can't something be done to keep them out.

Many years ago, when I was teaching in Colorado, I was driving East during the summer in my old Chevy carry-all, driving straight through, sleeping in the car. One night, driving on the New York Thruway somewhere near Rochester, I became too sleepy to drive safely any more and looked for a place to stop. There were no turn-offs or rest areas near, but at one point there was a big grassy stretch beside the shoulder, so I pulled far off the road, got out, and went to sleep beside the car. I was soon awakened and startled by a light shining in my eyes. It was a state trooper. He asked what I was doing there. I said that I was driving cross country, had become too sleepy to drive, and had stopped for a rest. He said harshly that I couldn't sleep by the side of the road. There seemed no reason for this; it was about three in the morning, there was virtually no traffic, and I was at least 150 feet from the edge of the highway. I said that I was afraid I might fall asleep while driving. He said, again harshly, "If you have to sleep, go to a motel." This seemed to sum it up; he was drumming up a little business for the local motel owners.

What we need are more of the kinds of summer campgrounds one finds in Europe, where travelers, driving or hitchhiking, can spend the night. These are often not beautiful, the tents are packed in tight, but it is an inexpensive way to spend the night, and it does make it possible for people with little money to see a lot of Europe.

There are things we could do to make hitchhiking easier and safer. Some hitchhikers try to pick up rides at places where stopping could cause an accident. But if hitchhiking were legal we could provide many more safe places to hitch from. Bulletin boards at colleges or at conferences attended by young people often carry much information about people looking for rides or willing to give them. At one college there is a very large map of the U.S., with states in outline, and on each major city a hook. Anyone planning to drive to a city puts a tag on the hook, telling when he is leaving, how many passengers he can carry, how to get in touch with him. But these information exchanges are mostly limited to colleges or places where college students hang out. We need something like this for people, young or old, who are not students. In many parts of the country learning exchanges are springing up, to help people exchange information and skills. Perhaps they could also find ways to exchange information about travel.

Travelers also need cheap places to rest and sleep. Europe is full of youth hostels. In 1953 I made a 1,500-mile bicycle trip most of the way from Paris to Rome, and on many nights I stayed in these hostels for about twenty-five cents a night, perhaps a little more in some of the fancier ones. A country that wanted to make it easy for people of any age without much money to travel could find or make very simple places where travelers could lay down their sleeping bags, blankets, or whatever, get a night's sleep, wash up, and continue. In 1953 a number of the Italian railroad stations had what they called an *albergo diurno*—a day hotel. They were a real blessing to travelers, above all in hot weather. In the *albergo diurno* were places to sit and relax, places to wash up, public showers, and cots and beds on which you could rest or sleep for an hour or a night. I have seen such facilities in several airports—in Edmonton in Canada, Amsterdam, and Copenhagen. They charged a fee, but much less than it would have cost people to go to a regular hotel.

If children could travel alone without their parents' permission, might they not get lost? Yes, they might. Adults get lost right now. It may be a nuisance, but not a tragedy or disaster. As long as a child knows how to get in touch with his home, or with friends, or as long as he has on or with him his name and address, being lost or confused for a while will do him no harm. Someone might ask, suppose he didn't know how to get in touch with home or friends, then what? We can only say that a child who would travel far without that much information is so reckless and foolish that even now the law and his parents can probably not keep him out of trouble. In any case, here, as in everything else I propose, the state can only provide choices; beyond a certain point they cannot guarantee that once these choices are made nothing will go wrong. Also, we have to ask how a child as reckless as the one imagined would have enough money to travel or would be able to get himself to a bus station or airport or would be able to get tickets.

Many adults traveling today are a great deal more helpless than most of the children who might want to travel. On planes I have seen total paralytics who had to be lifted out of their seats into wheel chairs and wheeled out of the plane, people who spoke no English at all, blind people. They cannot travel without help; but we do not forbid them to travel, and we make it easy for them to get what help they need. We do not assign them to compulsory helpers. To a large degree there is nothing that can be done to change the fact that the world is a large, varied, strange, confusing place. By providing better signs, maps, and sources of information, we could and should make it easier for people of any age to travel, even within their own city. Our society need not be as opaque as it is. But we cannot make the whole world as easy for a child to get around as his own house or neighborhood. That it is not as easy is the point of travel. Many children, even if asked by their parents to take a long journey by themselves, perhaps to see another relative, would be afraid, would not want to, might flatly refuse. Such children should and will stay home. The question of the *right* of such children to travel alone without their parents' permission will not come up; they could not be made to.

To some it will seem as if giving children the right to travel (and do other things) without their parents' permission would weaken the authority of the parents. We should note once more the distinction between natural authority, which rests on greater skill, knowledge, experience, courage, commitment, or concern, and that authority which rests only on force, the power to threaten, punish, and hurt. Nothing that I propose here can lessen the natural authority of the parent over the child or the old over the young; indeed it will strengthen such natural authority as exists.

Children are not indifferent to this natural authority. They get from it their sense of place in the world, a base from which they can move out in wider and wider circles. Their trust in and need for this authority are very strong, resilient, and persistent. Often, when a parent punishes—perhaps even spanks—a child, the hurt and angry child for a while shuns the parent. Usually not for long, though. Soon the child begins to make peace overtures—and it is almost always the child who makes them. Perhaps it is best that we let him make them, give him time to decide that he wants to, not press our contrition (if we feel any) too quickly on him. The child comes around—if he is little, quickly; if older, a bit more slowly—to try to make friends again. Wise and loving parents accept this offering with open arms, meet it in the same spirit. Others hold out, demand further repentance, demand that the child prove himself worthy. This is a most serious mistake. But a parent can make this mistake many times, can turn down a great many peace offerings from a child, before a child will finally and reluctantly decide that there is no use making any more peace offers, no one will respond, the only thing to do is avoid trouble if he can.

Suppose a child wants to travel and the parents do not want him to. We have to try to imagine the living family itself. One day the child says he would like to take a trip. If in this family there is still mutual love and respect, hence natural authority, the older people won't begin by saying the child's idea is wrong or silly. They will encourage him to talk about where he wants to go, when, how, and why. If they don't think the trip is a good idea, they will say why. Such discussions take place right now, when children ask their parents to let them go somewhere or do something. But even if a child did not need his parents' permission, he would want their approval and would spend some time trying to convince them, and they to convince him, before the question arose of who had the final right to decide.

Once I heard an eleven-year-old telling his mother he wanted to take a two- or three-day camping trip in the mountains with two friends. She raised all kinds of doubts and worries. At that time of year there were many thunderstorms in the mountains, hence the danger of lightning. Did he mind the possibility of storms? No, he didn't. Did he and his friends know enough to stay out of exposed places, high places, when there was an electrical storm or away from things that might attract lightning, like very tall trees or phone or power poles? What about keeping dry? How much clothing did they want to carry in? It grew very cold at night, colder than they realized. Did they have good enough sleeping bags? What about cooking? What would they eat? What would they do to keep themselves occupied for three days? And so the discussion went, for many days. Mother and son each brought up points, argued against the other's, made concessions. They were able to do this because he knew that she did not want to prevent him from camping but valued his adventurousness and competence. Her authority was persuasive because it was natural and not merely based on power.

The trip was finally okayed, then postponed one day because it looked very stormy. Eventually they worked out a compromise—yes, you can go, if you do this and if you make sure to bring that and so on. As it happened, many unforseen things went wrong. Both nights on the mountain, because of fog, or darkness catching them unawares, the campers slept away from their tent. They were often much colder and wetter than they had expected. If campers and mothers had known in advance all the things that were going to go wrong, there might have been no trip. As it was, the boys came down saying that there were a thousand things that they never thought of until they were actually camping. This is what experience is about.

But this scene would have been very much the same even if the boys had had the legal right to make this trip without their parents' permission. Except in families that in any real sense have ceased to exist, the young value many of the opinions of the old. They want the older people to think well of them.

Before this trip, the boys put up their tent on the grass by the house, just to be sure they knew how. In another family, a fairly young boy, before making a long camping trip with his father and older brother, slept out in the yard in a tent a number of times, to feel what it was like. On the whole, this is the way children like to meet new experiences —a little bit at a time. They do like to explore the unknown, but they are also cautious and conservative and don't want to explore all of it at once. No child, having never left home, is going to begin by thinking of taking a three-month trip to some place two thousand miles away. There is much truth in the old joke about the child who runs away from home but can't get past the corner because he doesn't know how to cross the street or comes home for dinner because he doesn't know any other way to get dinner. The child has to move a step at a time. The question is, shall we encourage and help these small steps out into the world or arbitrarily forbid them. People are more likely to take seriously their children's desires to explore, to discuss their projects respectfully, to raise only serious objections, and to make sensible compromises whenever possible, if they know that in case of a showdown they will not be able to prevent their children from doing what they want to do.

If we knew that children could, whenever they wished, make themselves independent of us, we would have every reason to help them prepare for this independence, and they would be sooner ready for it. A child who knows that wherever he goes an adult will take him will not pay much attention to how he goes there, and the adult will not have any reason to show him. How much better it would be if we urged the child to look and notice how he gets wherever he goes. A mother and seven-year-old child I know here in Boston are beginning to play an interesting game. When walking home, once they get past all the dangerous intersections, they split up, and each goes home by a different route. It is not a race but an experiment to find many different ways of getting home. Through this game, the child will get to know her neighborhood, and a larger and larger neighborhood, better and better. Or on small journeys, we might make the child the guide and say that we will only move where he tells us to go, as if we were a stranger or blind. Or an adult and child might go on an exploring walk, the child leading the way, going anywhere he felt like but not having to worry about getting lost because the adult could always take over on the trip home. All of these things we could do with children now.

City children do, of course, learn to get around, at least to certain places—many of them tend, for safety, to stick pretty close to home. But even when they explore further, go downtown, there is too often a sense of doing it in defiance of adult authority. There is surely a big difference between how it feels to explore a city, or a country, as forbidden territory and how it feels to explore it as a larger neighborhood in which you are welcome, *your* city, *your* country, *your* world.

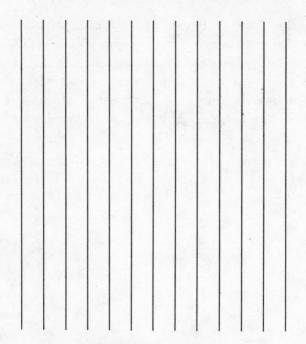

21. THE RIGHT TO CHOOSE ONE'S GUARDIAN

I would like to make available to young people these three choices: (1) to live, as they now do, as dependents under the care and control of their parents (natural or adoptive)—what I will call primary guardians; (2) to live as dependents but under the care and control of people, other than their parents, *of their own choosing,* in short, to choose what I will call secondary guardians; (3) to live as fully independent, financially and legally responsible citizens. In this chapter I would like to discuss in more detail the second of these three choices.

Even today the children of upper-middle-class or wealthy parents spend much of their lives, and more and more as they grow older, not with their parents but with people who are, as the law says, *in loco parentis*—in the place of the parent. Rich people do not have to bear much of the pain and strain of living with young people who have become too big to be children but whom society will not allow to be anything else. They buy secondary guardians for their children. Most people cannot afford this. I want these secondary guardians to be much more widely, readily, and cheaply available so that any young person who wanted to could make use of them. Even more important, I want *the child himself* to have the right to seek them out and choose them. These secondary guardians, chosen by the child, could be of two kinds: (1) individual, an older person or family, or (2) collective, some sort of group or community.

Let me try to make more clear this distinction between primary and secondary guardians. The relationship of secondary guardian would be voluntary and provisional, entered into by the mutual agreement of the child and secondary guardians, either of whom would have the right to end the agreement and the relationship. They might make this agreement (as the law says) *sine die,* that is, without naming a time at which it would end, and continue in the relationship until either (or both) chose to end it. Or they might make the agreement for a stated amount of time—a month, a year, or whatever—at which point they could decide whether they wanted to continue. But even in this case either party would have the right to end the agreement at any time they chose.

This would be somewhat like the pact that a student makes with a university. The agreement is for a fixed period of time—in the case of an undergraduate college it is four years—and the understanding is that if no one says anything to the contrary the student will be there until he graduates. But the student has at all times the right to leave if he chooses, and the college has at all times and for various causes the right to tell him to leave. The difference is that, since it has accepted the student's money, and also for other reasons, the college usually has to make known, and perhaps defend, its reasons for asking the student to leave. A secondary guardian, like the child himself, would not have to show cause for ending the relationship. Whatever his reasons might be, he would not have to tell or justify them to any third parties.

The relationship of primary guardian, on the other hand, would not be voluntary or provisional. A child's parents, whether natural or adoptive, would be his primary guardians. At least until the child reached his majority, they could not for any reason end this relationship. The child might choose to leave home, might choose to look for and live with other guardians, might even for a while live as an independent citizen. But if for whatever reason he decided that he wanted to return to his primary guardians and again live as their dependent, they could not refuse him. In short, this would not be a mutual or reciprocal obligation. For everyone designated by the law as a minor, there would always be someone who would be obliged to take responsibility for him if no one else wanted to. Some might say, it's not fair that the child's parents should be stuck with such a one-way obligation. But they have this obligation now, and it is fair because they brought the child into the world—or in the case of adoptive parents, they agreed to act as if they had.

Some might ask, why would anybody choose to be the primary rather than the secondary guardian of a child? One answer is that the relationship of secondary guardian, as I said before, must be entered into by the mutual choice of guardian and child. If a child is too young to make that choice, a baby or an infant, whoever wants him must be a primary guardian, must take on the responsibility of a natural parent.

Some might point out that even today primary guardians, parents of children, can in a pinch say to the law, "We can't manage this young person any longer, we don't want him in the house. Take him away and do something with him." In most cases, the law obligingly puts the young person in jail. I propose that it offer the young person other choices, to find other guardians or to live as an independent citizen. But, to take a very tough and I think, unlikely, case, suppose a child refused to live as an independent citizen and would not or could not find any secondary guardians who would be willing to have him and suppose his parents still insisted that they could not manage him—what then? In that case, I suppose the state could take over the care of the young person and put him in some sort of institution. In such a society the institutions of the state would almost certainly be much more humane than they are here and now. And the parents might have a much heavier burden of proof than they have now to show that they should be released from their primary guardianship. Or, the state might say to the young person, since you refuse to be dependent, we are going to declare you independent, whether you like it or not.

As long as a child was living with other people as his secondary guardians, they would be *in loco parentis,* as responsible for his acts as if they were his parents or as his parents would be today. Suppose a child did something very wrong or committed some crime while living with secondary guardians. They would be in part responsible for that act. They could say to the child, "If you are going to do things like this we don't want you living with us any more; find someone else or go back to your parents." But by ending their guardianship they would not end whatever their responsibility might be for what the child did when they were his guardians. In the same way, if a child committed some wrong or crime while living as an independent citizen, he could not shift the responsibility for this onto his parents merely by saying, "I want to come back and live with you."

The point of all I am proposing is that until they reached the age at which the law declared them (ready or not) to be adults and therefore full citizens, young people, instead of having to be dependent on people they did not choose and may not like, could move either toward a chosen dependency or toward independence. They could either choose their guardians and rulers, or could choose to have none. And they could move in and out of these states and so make a more gradual and less painful entry into the world.

All this may sound very abstract, but it needn't be. What I propose is only something that many people have already done without giving any fancy name to it. When I was small I used to spend parts of the summer visiting my grandparents in Grand Rapids, Michigan. I always had a good time there. I loved them and they me, and I made friends with other young people my age in the neighborhood. One summer, when I was eleven, my grandparents and I thought that it would be fun for us all if I could spend the whole winter with them. It seemed like such a strange idea—my grandfather was then about eighty—that at first we hardly dared imagine that it might be possible. But we finally got up the nerve to write my parents asking if it would be all right.

Back came the telegram: *Yes you may stay for winter.* And so I did, for one of the happiest years of my growing up.

Much more recently friends of mine in Boston had as their guest and ward for a year a boy who had been going to a school in Boston and wanted to stay there while his parents spent a year in a foreign country. The arrangement was fine for everyone. There must be many people, whose own children have long since grown up, who like young people and would be glad to have one living with them for a while, perhaps a year, perhaps more or less. Or some families with children might do some swapping. Even in the happiest of families there comes a time in the life of a child when he can hardly bear his family any more, or they him. Years ago a friend of mine, with a large and generally happy family of his own, told me, "John, if you ever get a family, there's one thing you should know. No matter how well you get along with your children when they are little, there is going to come a time when they will have no use for you, and you should be ready for it." Since then I have seen this many times, and often with previously very affectionate and happy children.

During my early teens, like many other young people, I was not always on the very best of terms with my parents. A close friend of mine was in the same situation; when I went to his house, he always seemed to be in some sort of hot water. But his parents liked me, and my parents liked him. It would probably have been good for all of us if he could have lived for a while with my family, and I for a while with his. In time the novelty would have worn off; his parents would have begun to see faults in me, and I in them, and the same with him and my family. The parents would have learned that their children's faults were not unique, and the same for the children. When we returned to our original relationships they would probably have gone more smoothly.

Sometimes a child not much liked or loved in one place would be much more so in another. One child I know is right now not very popular at home but an absolute joy to another family, who would be delighted to have her with them, even for as much as a year or more. There is no *necessary* reason why parents should like their own children best, or like them at all; they might prefer someone else's. Why not make it more easy for both adults and children to find those of the other group that they do like and to spend more time with them.

Groups, communities, organizations, could also be secondary guardians. Some examples of this exist right now. One of the largest is the armed forces. Its relationship to the people in it is in many ways that of a parent to child. It supplies all their basic needs—clothing, food, shelter; it tells them what to do; and it takes responsibility for their acts. If one of them gets in trouble away from the ship or base, the military police pick him up and say to the regular civilian police, "We'll take care of it." Colleges and universities are in a like relationship with their students, though less than they used to be. They supply them food and shelter, control many parts of their lives, and take legal responsibility for what they do, at least on campus. The boarding schools and camps that younger children go to are other examples, though in these the regular staff doubles as police. We have also YMCAs, YWCAs, YMHAs, and so forth, low-cost dormitories that can be found in many ski resorts; overnight huts on many hiking trails; shelters for runaways that churches and other groups have set up in many cities; short-term and low-cost accommodations to take care of summer visitors in

Copenhagen and other European cities popular with the young.

With these in mind we can imagine a group or network of organizations, communities, facilities, in which for very little money or even none at all young people could live under the loose supervision of some older people who would be responsible for them. Thus, it might be possible for a young person, if he wanted to live away from home for a while and could not find another family to act as his guardians, to sign up as a dependent of one of these groups. Indeed many young people, perhaps because of unhappy experiences in their original families or for other reasons, might prefer a less personal relationship with a different kind of community —the sort of thing children get when they go to camp or boarding school.

Alternative or free schools like Summerhill, Lewis-Wadhams, the Collins Brook School in Maine, the LEAP school in New York City, or any one of a number of others, could well be considered such communities. As a matter of fact, Neill always insisted that Summerhill *was* first and above all a community and only to a lesser degree a school, which it had to be because the law will not yet allow young people to live in a community unless it calls itself a school and makes certain school-like motions. And LEAP (Lower East Side Action Project) *began* as a community, a home away from home for young people of the neighborhood, who only later organized a school (among many other projects) because this is what they wanted. Many of these communities might even work better, might serve more people for less money, if they could exist frankly as communities without the burden of having to act like a school and to some degree carry out the inhumane and improper functions of schools—try to make

213

children learn what their elders want them to learn, get them into college, make sure they later get good jobs, succeed, and so forth. If the young people at these communities wanted some learning facilities and resources they could plan, run, and organize these as they chose. Some of these communities would be better for young people if they were not just for young people but for people of all ages. They might be still better if they had some kind of central purpose of their own, a farm, crafts, a small manufacturing business, music, theatre —in short, if they were a collection of people with a common concern.

The book *The Teacher Was The Sea* by Michael S. Kaye (Links Books, New York) is a very good, honest, and perceptive description of how one such community was formed, grew, and changed. It began as the Pacific High School, an alternative school near Palo Alto. But the longer people lived and worked in it, the more clearly, and often painfully, they learned that they could not meet the deepest needs of the young people there or establish truly honest and helpful relationships between younger and older people until they gave up the pretense that they were a school and became instead simply a community in which people of different ages lived and worked. Indeed, no writers have better described the hopeless contradiction of trying to run more or less conventional academic classes in a "free" high school.

Such communities, like all communities, would have their own rules, with perhaps some special rules for young people living there as dependents—a time for coming in at night, rules about quiet, perhaps a rule that dependents planning to stay away for a night or more would have to let the people in charge know where they were going. And such a community would have the same right as any other secondary guardian to end the relationship with the young person, tell him to leave if they found him too difficult or unpleasant to deal with. Some may see a contradiction here. But in a voluntary community there is no contradiction at all between freedom and rules. If you come of your own free will, and truly have the option to stay or go, then the community has a right to say to you, "If you want to stay here these are the things you have to do, and if you don't want to do them you can leave." In some communities like Summerhill and many others, these rules can be discussed and remade in open meetings; in others, they might be more or less fixed. I think a community should have a right to say to a visitor, "You have to live here for a while, show a lasting interest in the place, make a contribution to it, share our concerns, before we give you a voice in changing our rules." There could be great variety here.

Many of these communities might, and perhaps should, require that everyone living in them do some of the work to keep them running. This is good in itself and would help to keep the cost down. Some shelters might not have such a requirement; they would be more like the Y, or a very inexpensive hotel or even some of the large youth hostels I once stayed in, with a permanent staff of their own. Places that did not require residents to share in the work, and therefore had to pay to get it done, could fairly charge a higher price. So a young person could stay in a very inexpensive place where he had to do some of the work, or a somewhat more expensive place where he did not. Most would probably prefer the former.

Who would set up such places? Who would pay for them? Who would work in them? I can only suggest some answers here. When we think of institutions now run by the state, and the kind of people who too often work in them, it gives us pause. Will running these shelters become the kind of industry that running the schools or other institutions has become? Will there be, as in schools, the needless and wasteful racket of training, credentialing, certifying, and so forth? We should be able to prevent this. The difference between present institutions and the kinds of communities I am proposing is that most of the institutions now run by the state are a kind of jail. People do not choose to go into them and cannot choose to leave. They are there because other people, for reasons of their own, put them there, and they stay until other people, again for their own reasons, decide to let them out. This invites abuse and tyranny. But if the people in communities can leave if they don't like them, those who run them will have to run them to suit their clients, or have no clients.

How these places might be financed will depend in part on whether the society in which they exist guarantees a minimum income to all persons, including the young. If it does, the operating costs of shelters or communities could and should be borne by the people using them. This is the best way to make sure that they are really serving the people they mean to serve. If on the other hand, young people do not have the right to a guaranteed minimum income, then these shelters will have to get their money in other ways. Some will come from private organizations or from contributions or fees. Most will probably come from the state.

There are, broadly, two possibilities here. In Denmark the law now says that if a group of about ten or more families can start their own school and keep it running for a year, from then on the state will pay about eighty-five percent of the school's operating costs. The people running the school must take care of capital expenses. A government might make a similar offer to people wanting to start a youth shelter or community. On the other hand, and particularly if young people have their own money, it might be best to have the state pay a large part of the capital costs of these shelters—building, renovation, equipment, furniture—and then allow the operating costs to be met by the people living there. Or perhaps the state might offer a choice of these two.

Who would work in such places? Right now there are many more young people trying to get jobs in free schools or adventure playgrounds or other kinds of voluntary communities than there are paying jobs for them. So there is no reason to suppose that we would find it hard to staff these communities, particularly if everyone had a minimum income and therefore did not need to be paid, or paid very much, for their work. Perhaps the state might add a small salary to whatever the institution or organization itself could pay. Or in exchange for their work it might guarantee them a certain income.

On the whole, rather than have these institutions, or any helping institutions, run by and supported by the state, I would prefer to have the state give people money and let them organize and support the institutions they needed and wanted—the principle of the voucher plan, but greatly extended. Perhaps the state might require for such places some minimum standards of health and safety. But even this has its dangers. Too often, as in the case of building codes, day care, and so on, the effect of "standards" is to price a needed service out of the reach of the people who need it most and to turn it from a human activity into a commodity and a monopoly out of which specialists make profitable careers. The state (in most cases, the cities) does not enforce its own codes of health and safety in the housing in which most poor people have to live. But it has often used these same codes as an excuse to shut down schools or other institutions which these same poor people are trying to organize to help themselves.

There is no reason why living quarters in these shelters or communities should be anything but very simple. Larry and Michele Cole and their students at the LEAP school in New York City designed some very ingenious portable, foldable bed, storage, and study units for young people who wanted to live at the school. These can be folded up into a very large box, or they can open out to make a small private room, or they can be combined to make double or triple rooms, or joined together in any way the students like. These boxes are not at all expensive to build and can be put into any large room—the LEAP school used to be a store.

The danger I fear and want at all costs to avoid is that there would be such demand for these places that a new industry and bureaucracy, like that of the schools, would spring up, perhaps intelligent and responsive at first but in time more and more rigid, rule-bound, defensive, and self-serving. It would be vital to find ways to keep these organizations small, informal, and decentralized. And, as with the schools in Denmark, people who were not satisfied with what existed should always have the right to make something new for themselves. The needs of people for shelter, a place to stay, and companionship are very basic ones, and no one should be allowed to get a monopoly—professional, legal, or otherwise—over their supply.

Would a society good enough to *make* such institutions *need* them? Yes, though perhaps less than the societies we have now. Even in the most sensible and humane society, the young will need change, independence, adventure, the chance to travel and meet new people, and above all to get away from their families so that they may come back later and meet and get to know them again, to some degree as new people. And this would do the families themselves good. Like rich people now, they could have their devout but vain wish, to be for at least a while rid of their restless and impatient young.

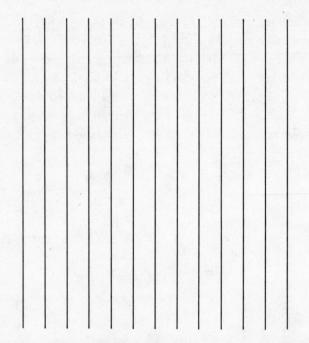

22. THE RIGHT TO A GUARANTEED INCOME

If the only way for most people to have a decent livelihood in a given society is to have a job, and if there are many more people than jobs, then clearly many people will have to depend on some jobholder for support. Today about half the women in the country, many of the old, and all of the young are in this position. As long as they remain so, to talk about their independence or their equal rights is to some extent unrealistic. If they can only get the things they need from someone who holds a job, then that jobholder or breadwinner is going to feel he has the right to tell them what to do. And to a large degree, whatever the law may say, he will be right. They have little choice but to do what he tells them, because they have nowhere else to go.

In our society when we talk about equal rights for women or children we are necessarily talking mostly of the upper-middle and wealthy classes, where women and even the young are more likely to have some money of their own or where it will be easier for them to get some of whatever jobs there are or where they can more easily get help from other people who do have money. Most people do not have these choices. Lower-middle-class and poor women and children will remain locked into dependency on some jobholder unless they can have some sure source of income of their own.

For this reason the right of everyone to choose to be independent can hardly be fully meaningful except in a society that gives everyone some guaranteed minimum income. Why such an income should be paid, how large it should be, how it should financed, what are the psychological and political obstacles to attaining it, what might be effective strategies for overcoming these obstacles—all of these are questions which deserve more space than I can give here. What I propose is that such an income should be guaranteed, not just to all adults, male or female, single or married, but to all children as well, down to an early age—as early as the child wants to receive it. For obviously the right to leave home, to travel, to seek other guardians, to live where they choose, and alone if they choose, cannot be an active or meaningful right for most young people unless they can get the money they need to live. Some will object that this much financial independence might weaken family ties. But the state ought not to use the threat of poverty as a glue to hold the family or other personal relationships together.

If a child is living as a dependent, an older guardian paying for his shelter, clothing, food, and other necessities, should some of the child's income go to the older person to help meet these expenses; and if so, how much? If the child was living under a mutual agreement with a secondary guardian of his own choosing, they would probably have discussed and agreed upon this. If the guardian had not much money, he would probably say to the child, "If you want to come to live here you have to pay so many dollars for your own support." If the guardian was richer, he might not require this. If child and guardian later grew dissatisfied with this part of their agreement, they could take it up again. In a pinch, the guardian could always say, "If you won't pay that much money, we can't afford to keep you, and you can't live here." It does seem unlikely that people who in every other respect wanted to live together would fall out on this point.

But the parent, the primary guardian, could not tell the child to pay so much or get out. How then would he receive a fair share of the child's income? What would be a fair share? Would these matters be written into law? For reasons that are by now probably clear, I would prefer not. Perhaps there might be a flat provision that if a child was living with a primary guardian some percentage of his income would be paid directly to the guardian. If guardian and child then wanted to change this division, they could work it out between them.

Some might ask if every member of a family received an income of his own, each filling out his own tax form and receiving a tax credit, might this not lead to endless arguments about how this money was to be pooled or shared and how much each member of the family should contribute to the family expenses? Would it not be better, as at present, for everyone to put their income into the family pool, to treat the family as a single economic unit? In the situation I propose families might indeed argue about money. But the way we avoid this danger today seems even worse. It is all very well to say that the family is an economic unit and that everyone in it contributes all their income to the family expenses. In practice this often means that all the property and income of the family belongs to the (usually male) head of the family and that the other members of the family have to bargain or beg for money for their personal needs or use. In other words, we have already the problem of how family resources should be divided. The difference is that today the dependent members of the family have to bargain or beg from a weak and unequal position; unless they work, they do not have any income or right to any. If everyone received his own guaranteed income and either paid taxes or received a tax credit, there might well be fewer family disputes about money rather than more. But such technical questions as these will have to be worked out politically; they can't be and don't need to be decided here.

One final point should be made. It is above all the threat and fear of poverty that locks many people into dependency on others. But no nation, even if it provides everyone with a guaranteed income, will overcome poverty or reduce the fear of it unless it constantly lowers, or at the very least holds steady, the minimum amount of income that people need to live decently. The real test of the quality of life in a nation, as in a community, is how well the poorest people in it live.

23. THE RIGHT TO LEGAL AND FINANCIAL RESPONSIBILITY

Young people should have two rights they do not now have. The first is the right to the full and equal protection of the law. The second is the right to choose to live as a fully legally and financially responsible citizen.

By the first I mean that children should receive all the protection against arbitrary action by others or by the state that due process and other provisions of the law give to adults and that in any situation the law should treat them no worse than it would an adult. Neither of these is now the case. Most people think that our law treats children more kindly and gently than adults because we want to make allowances for their youth and inexperience. The fact is that most of the time we treat them much *worse*. Large numbers of young people are in jails—that is, institutions which they are not free to leave and in which they are as a rule callously, brutally, and cruelly treated—not because they have *done* anything at all but because the state cannot find anyone who will give them the "love, concern, and so on" that they supposedly need. Still more young people are in jail for doing things which, if done by adults, are not crimes or even wrongs. And many young people who are in jail for real crimes are there much longer than would be an adult who had committed the same crime.

Out of a flood of examples I pick a few. From a story, "Children's Rights: The Latest Crusade," in *Time* magazine of December 25, 1972:

> Young Gerald Gault may have thought it was just a joke. He telephoned a housewife who lived near by in Globe, Ariz. and made what the Supreme Court subsequently called "remarks or questions of the irritatingly offensive, adolescent sex variety." The boy had no lawyer, the housewife never publicly testified, no hearing transcripts were kept and no appeal was possible. Gault could have received a *maximum jail term of two months* [italics mine] if he had been an adult; since he was 15, he was committed to the State Industrial School until he became 21. Two years passed before the Supreme Court turned him loose in 1967 . . .

Elsewhere in this same story we read:

> . . . Consider the case of Pam, now 16. Her mother was struggling to make ends meet after her husband deserted her, and Pam was difficult to handle. So the mother gave

her up to the state. "Pam is very bright and fantastically sensitive," explains Chicago Attorney Patrick Murphy, "but she's not very attractive. So she was sent out to a foster home for a year, then back to the delinquent home, [My note: why do we have to keep calling these jails "homes"?] then to Elgin State Hospital. She's gotten into fights because other kids taunted her about her looks. At Elgin, things got worse [My note: what does that phrase cover up?], so they tied her to her bed for 28 days. When they let her go, she hit a matron, so they put her back in restraints for another 30 days. By this time she really needs psychotherapy."

I would like to suggest instead that what she really needs is for the state to get its damned hands off her. The story goes on:

. . . In Chicago's Cook County Juvenile Court, the 28,740 cases handled last year included only 3,500 serious offenses but fully 9,200 instances of parental neglect and juvenile runaways. In many cases, the runaways had reason to flee—cruelty, indifference, or neglect. "Parents are allowed to beat children," says Stanford Katz, "and no action may be taken unless the child is seriously injured." . . . In Massachusetts, one intractable 15-year-old in a foster home was taken to court after she disobeyed her foster parents' rule *that she could not talk to boys.* [Italics mine] She was held to be a "depraved child" but the court could not decide on any punishment.

"Depraved." "Punishment." All this because she would not obey an order not to talk to boys. Perhaps we need to write into law that children have a right to talk to whomever they please. All this surpasses belief. But the story continues, and let me add that the following incident is increasingly common:

. . . Chicago was shocked recently by the case of Johnny Lindquist, age six. He was living happily in a foster home after his parents declared they could not provide for him. Then his parents changed their minds, and social workers [My note: professional helpers] returned the boy—even though he expressed fear of his father. Four months later, according to police, the father beat the boy senseless. Johnny's skull was crushed. After lying for four weeks in a coma, he died. As a result, an Illinois senate committee has been holding hearings on whether to change child-care laws to resemble those of California, where "due weight" is given to the child's own wishes about custody if he "is of sufficient age and capacity to reason."

I do not know what action the Illinois Legislature will take on this bill. I doubt they will pass it. What is more important, had such a law been on the books, I doubt that it would have made the slightest difference in the case of Johnny Lindquist or others like him. In the U.S. today what official body, what group of professional helpers and protectors of children, would agree that a six-year-old was "of sufficient age and capacity to reason?" And yet this is exactly the point of the story, and a point that *Time* magazine wholly missed. In this matter *it was Johnny who was right*. His judgement was more accurate and his reasoning better than that of the state and its adult experts. *He knew*. They did not. Will we listen any more attentively to the next six-year-old who tells us that he knows what he wants and needs? It's not likely.

. . . Lawyer-Psychologist Joseph Goldstein of Yale Law School opposes legalistic custodial laws that assign orphaned children to their nearest blood relatives. . . . [he] prefers laws that would [allow] the judge discretion to assign the children to a distant relative or even a close friend who is fond of them.

That would certainly be an improvement. But how about allowing the child some discretion? Why does he get no say in the matter?

At the end of this article we come right back to where we started with this statement, which I would call extraordinary except that it is what most people think and would say:

> The challenge will be to define rights in a way that expands the child's protection against abuse without undermining the psychic benefits of parental authority. "There is no way the government can supply the 24-hour, seven-day, 52-week care of a good parent."

Nonsense! In the first place, no parent supplies or in the history of the world ever did supply such care; people have other things to do. No child (unless perhaps in an iron lung) needs such care; if he had it, it might well drive him crazy. Heaven protect children from people who have nothing to do in their lives but think of them. But beyond that, what *Time* asks, to expand protection against abuses of authority without diminishing authority, is impossible, a contradiction in terms. There can be no adequate protection against the abuse of authority, of parents or the state, except to give the victim the right to escape it.

The authority that *Time* has in mind when it talks about the "psychic benefits of parental authority" is not natural authority but only the power to compel, threaten, punish, and hurt. The fact is that children can be and are regularly punished, by parents and the law, for any of the reasons, and the same reasons for which slaves used to be punished—for talking back, for "disrespect," for disobedience, for being at large without permission, for running away—in short, for doing anything that might imply that they think they have any freedom or rights at all.

Let us look here at part of a news story, headlined *Child Abuse Held a Leading Killer,* by Jane Brody in *The New York Times* of June 27, 1973:

Child abuse is believed to be the most common cause of death among small children in this country, a medical symposium was told last night.

Dr. Vincent J. Fontana, a national authority in the problem of child abuse, also said that this year alone, 50,000 children were expected to die and 300,000 to be permanently injured by maltreatment. . . .

Despite the prevalence of child abuse, he told the annual meeting of the American Medical Association, physicians tend to close their eyes to the problem, the Government fails to support prevention programs, and the public is generally unaware of the extent of child abuse, which, he said, seems to be approaching an epidemic. . . .

For every case that receives public attention, Dr. Fontana said, perhaps a dozen others go undetected or unreported.

"It is a false assumption that this is just a ghetto disease or done only by people who are mentally ill," Dr. Fontana told a news conference before his address. "Among the middle class, child battering is more often done behind closed doors. It usually doesn't get to a doctor's attention or if it does, the doctor protects the family by not reporting it and in the process fails to protect the child." . . .

Dr. Arthur Green, child psychiatrist at Downstate Medical Center in Brooklyn, said at the news conference that a study of 60 mothers who had abused their children showed the women to be lonely, immature, suspicious. untrusting persons with a multitude of problems.

"But most were not psychotic," he reported. "Rather, they tend to have a *neurotic dependence on the child, expecting the child to fulfill their needs, instead of the reverse. If such mothers feel they are rejected by the child or that the child is not performing according to expectations, they tend to abuse him*," Dr. Green said. [Italics mine]

As in talking about schools, and the right of children to choose to go or not to go to them, I do not want to argue about who is the best defender of the child, his parents or his institutional and professional protectors. Sometimes it is the parent who is most truly on the side of the child, trying to defend him against teachers, doctors, psychologists, or other experts who are doing him real harm. Just as often the shoe is on the other foot, and the employees of the state are trying to protect a child against a destructive parent. *Time*'s story makes it plain enough; how could it be plainer? Johnny Lindquist's father murdered *him;* Pam's institutional protectors tied *her* to a bed for 58 days (plus goodness knows what else—her life in the hands of the state is just beginning, who knows what it yet has in store for her?).

The point is that we cannot decide, once and for all, whether it is parents, teachers, counselors, psychologists, family courts, judges, or whatever, who know what is best for children. *In important matters, nobody can know better than the child himself.* You don't have to be very old or very smart to know your friends from your enemies, to know when people dislike you, are cruel to you, and hurt you. Any five-year-old knows the difference between a mean teacher and a nice one and is smart enough to want to get away from

230

the mean one. It is only adults who are stupid enough to think that the mean teacher is somehow doing the child some good. Not that the adults themselves willingly stick around people who are contemptuous and cruel to them. Not for a minute. It is only to other people, above all young people, that we say that pain doesn't really hurt, it really does you good. But a child should have the same right as anyone else to move away from whoever or whatever is hurting him and toward whatever he feels may help him.

On the matter of equal protection of the law, here are some other quotes, the first an article by Enid Nemy in *The New York Times* of November 3, 1973:

Beyond divorce cases, minors in New York generally are not allowed to bring a court action unless an adult acts for them.

. . . two major deficiencies in children's rights. One is the denial of the privilege to bring suit at any age. . . .

Mrs Uviler . . . is disturbed by court procedures used for nondeliquent minors known as Persons in Need of Supervision (PNS). "The child who has committed no law violation . . . the stubborn child, the incorrigible child . . . [My note: who may insist on her right to talk to boys.] should be removed from the judicial process. They are brought in mainly by overwhelmed parents who think they will get some help and their treatment is indistinguishable from that accorded to delinquents."

The brief prepared by Mrs. Pipel and Dr. Hoffman notes that under the present juvenile court system, a youth may be deprived of his freedom for longer periods than would an adult for a similar act.

From an article in *The Real Paper* (Boston) by Chuck

Frager, "Halfway to Reform; Jerry Miller Opened the Doors," January 24, 1972:

> . . . And a number of (Mass.) state judges are trying to get from the legislature the power to declare any juvenile "dangerous" and order his or her confinement in a locked setting for up to several months. [Says Miller, formerly head of the Mass. Division of Youth Services] "Now they will say that they would hardly ever use this authority, but if you look at their records the fact is that they used to say this about practically every kid that came before them."

From Howard James' book *Children in Trouble* (Pocket Books), which along with Larry Cole's *Our Children's Keepers* and Lois Forer's *No One Will Listen*,* tells us a great deal about how children are treated by the law and the institutions set up to "protect" them:

> Thousands of children—some as young as 7 or 8—spend months, even years, behind bars for offenses that would not put an adult in jail for an hour.

> The National Council on Crime and Delinquency estimates that "every year in the United States over 100,000 children from 7 to 17 inclusive are held in jails and jail-like places of detention. . . . the significance of this is not merely the large number held, or the fact that most of the jails in which they are detained are rated unfit for adult offenders by the Federal Bureau of Prisons' Inspections Service, but rather that many of these youngsters did not need to be detained in a secure facility in the first place." I have found, after reading case histories prepared by professionals, and after interviewing hundreds of children in trouble, that nearly every delinquent has had an inadequate home. Sometimes parents have serious

---

* This was spelled LISSEN by the author.

handicaps, like alcoholism. Often the child is rejected or thinks he is rejected. I have found hundreds who feel this way. Many blame themselves for parents' divorces. Or they have been beaten so badly and so often *that they feel totally unloved.* [Italics mine] Girls have been sexually molested by their fathers.

The words "beaten so badly and so often that they feel totally unloved" are not meant to be ironical. Mr. James is saying that with a perfectly straight face. For all I know the children may have said just those words in talking to him. Such words and such thinking are both odd and terrible. It would not take more than one bad beating to convince *me* that I was unloved, and if beatings are the price of "love," I can do without it.

Millard, a very talented 16-year-old . . . was jailed with various Atlanta hoodlums by the welfare department because he had arguments with his foster mother. Yet he had not broken the law. The woman simply decided she couldn't deal with a rebelling teen-ager. [P. 31]

It is rather common for boys to be homosexually assaulted by adults in jails. This happens frequently in Chicago and Philadelphia, among other cities. [P. 33]

The beating of children, or flogging with heavy straps, is common in these institutions. The people in charge explained this to James by saying that when they stop the beatings, the runaway rate goes up and the outraged public raises a stink until beatings and floggings are reinstated.

[Jim] was first sent to Marianna [Florida School for Boys] at age 12 and was held two years and two months. During that time he was hit by guards and was twice beaten with a

233

flogging strap, *one for fighting with a larger boy who was trying to force him into a homosexual act.* [Italics mine]

Marianna is one of the towns in which, according to Mr. James, the citizens demanded the reinstatement of flogging. Sometimes it almost seems as if many Americans, whose appetite for punishment and cruelty is not satisfied by the sadism of professional "sport" or of so many current films, books, and magazines, need to feel that people are being made to suffer in prison and get positive satisfaction rather than revulsion from hearing of these beatings and floggings. Are we using children not just as love objects but as hate objects, to work off our rage at the world?

Our mistreatment of children is often very expensive. One would hardly guess what it can cost to keep a child in an institution where he has almost no learning or recreational facilities, almost no contact with adults, where he eats inadequate food, sleeps on a cot in a bare cell, in a dormitory, or even out in a corridor, and where he is frequently abused, beaten, or assaulted by the guards. According to news reports in recent years, in the state of Massachusetts, depending a little on the institution, this treatment can cost as much as $10,000 to $14,000 a year! As the writer of one article on this subject pointed out, for that money a child could go to the most expensive boarding schools or colleges in the state and during vacation live in the best hotel in Boston or in any resort he chose. We talk about children not being able to make decisions or use judgement. Almost any eight-year-old with $12,000 a year to spend could do better for himself than the state and its army of police and protectors usually do for him. *Time* magazine, leading into its story about Johnny

Lindquist, said, "But younger children cannot simply be turned loose." To which I ask, in all seriousness, why not? If no one wants them, or there is no place they want to go, why can't we give them the money they would need to live on, a fraction of the money we would spend "caring" for them, and let them live their own lives—like the little Italian boys I spoke of, who did better for themselves in time of war and with no money at all than Johnny Lindquist, or the boy who was blinded at Willowbrook, or . . . but they are too many to mention.

I believe it was Fred Wiseman, the maker of documentary films (*Titicut Follies; High School; Law and Order; Basic Training; Hospital;* and others) who told me this story. Looking for a subject in making his documentary film *Juvenile Court*, he was investigating parts of the systems of "juvenile justice." At one point he found himself in a courtroom where three or four adults were discussing the case of a fifteen-year-old youth who had been brought before them. The experts, perhaps a judge, an attorney, a psychologist, and so on, were busily discussing what to do with the youth. Across the room sat the youth. Every so often he would raise his voice to say, "All I want is a fair trial, like anybody else gets. Just give me a fair trial." He might as well have saved his breath. He wasn't going to *get* a fair trial. He wasn't going to get *any* trial.

But this is exactly what I want for young people—the right to a fair trial, to all the protection of due process, and the right to bring suit. Of course many adults, if poor or from a minority group, do not get a fair trial either. Many such adults are in jail for many months or even a year or more, awaiting trial, because they cannot afford the excessive

235

bail which, in defiance of the Constitution, the judge has required of them. Those who can afford bail can usually not afford the enormous costs of an adequate defense. A man I know was unjustly fired from his job as school principal, mostly for being on too good terms with the students. He decided to fight the issue in court. When I saw him, and spoke at a meeting to raise money for his defense, he had already spent well over $5,000 and the case had not even come to court. On the whole, the law belongs to the rich, and justice is for those who can pay for it. But even poor adults get a better break than the young.

But I want more for the child than the right, in spite of being a child, to have all the protections of the law granted to adults. I want in addition the right to decide *not* to be a child, not to be dependent any longer on guardians of any kind, but to live as an independent, financially and legally responsible citizen. I want the right, in all respects, to escape from childhood.

What would it mean to give a young person full legal and financial responsibility? Just what it now means for adults. It would mean that he was accountable to his fellow citizens and the law for what he does. It would mean that he could sue others and be sued by them. It would mean that he could own, buy, and sell property, make contracts, establish credit, borrow money, and do all the other things an adult may now legally do.

Ideally young people should be able to make this choice at any age. As the case of other rights, it seems likely that if the barriers to citizenship come down, they will come down slowly, a year or two at a time.

People ask, "What would happen if a child, having assumed full financial responsibility, contracted debts he could not pay?" The answer is, just what would happen to anyone else. If he could not persuade his creditors to hold off, promising to pay later, they would take him to court or he would file a petition in bankruptcy. In this case the law would take his disposable property—motorcycle, skis, camping equipment, car, bicycle, stero set, whatever he owns—sell it for what they could get, and use the money to pay off his debts.

Since a young person, even if he had a job or was receiving a guaranteed income, would not be able to earn or have as much money as an older person—unless, of course, he was some kind of athletic or entertainment star—people would not be likely to lend him much money or extend him much credit. Just because the law says I *can* borrow money does not mean that anyone must lend it me. I still have to convince them that they will get it back. A child's credit would not be very good because his earning power would not be.

Could a child living as an independent citizen choose to continue to live with his parents? Yes, but only if they agreed. He would have to make the same bargain with them as any adult guest. If they liked his company and wanted him as a guest in the house, they could very well say, make yourself at home. But they would not be *obliged* to take him unless he chose to live again as their dependent.

It seems reasonable that people should not be able to change their minds too quickly about being independent. For one thing, the change would involve some record-keeping. Today, a person only has to show proof of age to show that he is an adult citizen. But if a twelve-year-old could choose to be a citizen he would have to get some sort of record or identification showing this—something like a passport, or Social Security card, or credit card. He would have to apply for this some time in advance, perhaps file certain forms with various local or other government officials. Similarly, if he wanted to give up his independence and return to being a dependent, he would have to notify people of this. There would be a procedure to go through. The taking on of citizenship by young people should not be a light act—too many people take it too lightly as it is.

Should younger people have to fulfill certain conditions in order to become citizens? Since most people get citizenship, full financial and legal responsibility, just by reaching a certain age, it may seem unfair to require others, just because they are younger, to fulfill certain conditions to get it. Yet a case can be made for asking people below a certain age to show that they understand some of the responsibilities and obligations they are undertaking. People have to pass a test before they can drive a car. Those who go to live in another country have to fulfill certain conditions to become citizens. It is certainly possible that young people wanting to be citizens might first have to take part in some meetings or discussions or pass a test. There is always the danger that this test would not be administered fairly. We would have to hope that a country enlightened enough to offer citizenship to its young would be honest enough not to try to cheat them out of it.

I am aware that what I have just said differs from what I said in the matter of voting. But I think the act of taking up the burden of citizenship, of assuming full legal and financial responsibility, can have much more serious personal consequences than the act of registering to vote. One can after all decide not to vote, and though one may regret a decision made in the voting booth, one cannot be fined, penalized, or jailed for it. For this reason it might be wise as well as fair to require that people below a certain age, applying to be citizens, show that at least to some degree they know what that means.

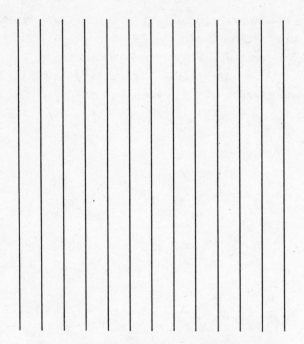

24. THE RIGHT TO CONTROL ONE'S LEARNING

Young people should have the right to control and direct their own learning, that is, to decide what they want to learn, and when, where, how, how much, how fast, and with what help they want to learn it. To be still more specific, I want them to have the right to decide if, when, how much, and by whom they want to be *taught* and the right to decide whether they want to learn in a school and if so which one and for how much of the time.

No human right, except the right to life itself, is more fundamental than this. A person's freedom of learning is part of his freedom of thought, even more basic than his freedom of speech. If we take from someone his right to decide what he will be curious about, we destroy his freedom of thought. We say, in effect, you must think not about what interests and concerns *you*, but about what interests and concerns *us*.

We might call this the right of curiosity, the right to ask whatever questions are most important to us. As adults, we assume that we have the right to decide what does or does not interest us, what we will look into and what we will leave alone. We take this right for granted, cannot imagine that it might be taken away from us. Indeed, as far as I know, it has never been written into any body of law. Even the writers of our Constitution did not mention it. They thought it was enough to guarantee citizens the freedom of speech and the freedom to spread their ideas as widely as they wished and could. It did not occur to them that even the most tyrannical government would try to control people's minds, what they thought and knew. That idea was to come later, under the benevolent guise of compulsory universal education.

This right of each of us to control our own learning is now in danger. When we put into our laws the highly authoritarian notion that someone should and could decide what all young people were to learn and, beyond that, could do whatever might seem necessary (which now includes dosing them with drugs) to compel them to learn it, we took a long step down a very steep and dangerous path. The requirement that a child go to school, for about six hours a day, 180 days a year, for about ten years, whether or not he learns anything there, whether or not he already knows it or could learn it faster or better somewhere else, is such a gross violation of civil liberties that few adults would stand for it. But the child who resists is treated as a criminal. With this requirement we created an industry, an army of people whose whole work was to tell young people what they had to learn and to try to make them learn it. Some of these people, wanting to exercise even more power over others, to be even more "helpful," or simply because the industry is not growing fast enough to hold all the people who want to get into it, are now beginning to say, "If it is good for children for us to decide what they shall learn and to make them learn it, why wouldn't it be good for everyone? If compulsory education is a good thing, how can there be too much of it? Why should we allow anyone, of any age, to decide that he has had enough of it? Why should we allow older people, any more than young, not to know what we know when their ignorance may have bad consequences for all of us? Why should we not *make* them know what they *ought* to know?"

They are beginning to talk, as one man did on a nationwide TV show, about "womb-to-tomb" schooling. If hours of homework every night are good for the young, why wouldn't they be good for us all—they would keep us away from the TV set and other frivolous pursuits. Some group of experts, somewhere, would be glad to decide what we all ought to know and then every so often check up on us to make sure we knew it—with, of course, appropriate penalties if we did not.

I am very serious in saying that I think this is coming unless we prepare against it and take steps to prevent it. The right I ask for the young is a right that I want to preserve for the rest of us, the right *to decide what goes into our minds.* This is much more than the right to decide whether or when or how much to go to school or what school you want to go to. That right is important, but it is only part of a much larger and more fundamental right, which I might call the

242

right to Learn, as opposed to being Educated, *i.e.*, made to learn what someone else thinks would be good for you. It is not just compulsory schooling but compulsory Education that I oppose and want to do away with.

That children might have the control of their own learning, including the right to decide if, when, how much, and where they wanted to go to school, frightens and angers many people. They ask me, "Are you saying that if the parents wanted the child to go to school, and the child didn't want to go, that he wouldn't have to go? Are you saying that if the parents wanted the child to go to one school, and the child wanted to go to another, that the child would have the right to decide?" Yes, that is what I say. Some people ask, "If school wasn't compulsory, wouldn't many parents take their children out of school to exploit their labor in one way or another?" Such questions are often both snobbish and hypocritical. The questioner assumes and implies (though rarely says) that these bad parents are people poorer and less schooled than he. Also, though he appears to be defending the right of children to go to school, what he really is defending is the right of the state to compel them to go whether they want to or not. What he wants, in short, is that children should be in school, not that they should have any choice about going.

But saying that children should have the right to choose to go or not to go to school does not mean that the ideas and wishes of the parents would have no weight. Unless he is estranged from his parents and rebelling against them, a child cares very much about what they think and want. Most of the time, he doesn't want to anger or worry or disappoint them. Right now, in families where the parents feel that they have some choice about their children's schooling, there is much bargaining about schools. Such parents, when their children are little, often ask them whether they want to go to nursery school or kindergarten. Or they may take them to school for a while to try it out. Or, if they have a choice of schools, they may take them to several to see which they think they will like the best. Later, they care whether the child likes his school. If he does not, they try to do something about it, get him out of it, find a school he will like.

I know some parents who for years had a running bargain with their children, "If on a given day you just can't stand the thought of school, you don't feel well, you are afraid of something that may happen, you have something of your own that you very much want to do—well, you can stay home." Needless to say, the schools, with their supporting experts, fight it with all their might—Don't Give in to Your Child, Make Him Go to School, He's Got to Learn. Some parents, when their own plans make it possible for them to take an interesting trip, take their children with them. They don't ask the school's permission, they just go. If the child doesn't want to make the trip and would rather stay in school, they work out a way for him to do that. Some parents, when their child is frightened, unhappy, and suffering in school, as many children are, just take him out. Hal Bennett, in his excellent book *No More Public School*, talks about ways to do this.

A friend of mine told me that when her boy was in third grade, he had a bad teacher, bullying, contemptuous, sarcastic, cruel. Many of the class switched to another section, but this eight-year-old, being tough, defiant, and stubborn, hung on. One day—his parents did not learn this until about two years later—having had enough of the teacher's meanness, he just got up from his desk and without saying a word, walked

244

out of the room and went home. But for all his toughness and resiliency of spirit, the experience was hard on him. He grew more timid and quarrelsome, less outgoing and confident. He lost his ordinary good humor. Even his handwriting began to go to pieces—it was much worse in the spring of the school year than in the previous fall. One spring day he sat at breakfast, eating his cereal. After a while he stopped eating and sat silently thinking about the day ahead. His eyes filled up with tears, and two big ones slowly rolled down his cheeks. His mother, who ordinarily stays out of the school life of her children, saw this and knew what it was about. "Listen," she said to him, "we don't have to go on with this. If you've had enough of that teacher, if she's making school so bad for you that you don't want to go any more, I'll be perfectly happy just to pull you right out. We can manage it. Just say the word." He was horrified and indignant. "No!" he said, "I couldn't do that." "Okay," she said, "whatever you want is fine. Just let me know." And so they left it. He had decided that he was going to tough it out, and he did. But I am sure knowing that he had the support of his mother and the chance to give it up if it got too much for him gave him the strength he needed to go on.

To say that children should have the right to control and direct their own learning, to go to school or not as they chose, does not mean that the law would forbid the parents to express an opinion or wish or strong desire on the matter. It only means that if their natural authority is not strong enough the parents can't call in the cops to make the child do what they are not able to persuade him to do. And the law may say that there is a limit to the amount of pressure or coercion the parents can apply to the child to deny him a choice that he has a legal right to make.

When I urge that children should control their learning there is one argument that people bring up so often that I feel I must anticipate and meet it here. It says that schools are a place where children can for a while be protected against the bad influences of the world outside, particularly from its greed, dishonesty, and commercialism. It says that in school children may have a glimpse of a higher way of life, of people acting from other and better motives than greed and fear. People say, "We know that society is bad enough as it is and that children will be exposed to it and corrupted by it soon enough. But if we let children go out into the larger world as soon as they wanted, they would be tempted and corrupted just that much sooner."

They seem to believe that schools are better, more honorable places than the world outside—what a friend of mine at Harvard once called "museums of virtue." Or that people in school, both children and adults, act from higher and better motives than people outside. In this they are mistaken. There are, of course, some good schools. But on the whole, far from being the opposite of, or an antidote to, the world outside, with all its envy, fear, greed, and obsessive competitiveness, the schools are very much like it. If anything, they are worse, a terrible, abstract, simplified caricature of it. In the world outside the school, some work, at least, is done honestly and well, for its own sake, not just to get ahead of others; people are not everywhere and always being set in competition against each other; people are not (or not yet) in every minute of their lives subject to the arbitrary, irrevocable orders and judgement of others. But in most schools, a student is every minute doing what others tell him, subject to their judgement, in situations in which he can only win at the expense of other students.

This is a harsh judgement. Let me say again, as I have before, that schools are worse than most of the people in them and that many of these people do many harmful things they would rather not do, and a great many other harmful things that they do not even see as harmful. The whole of school is much worse than the sum of its parts. There are very few people in the U.S. today (or perhaps anywhere, any time) in *any* occupation, who could be trusted with the kind of power that schools give most teachers over their students. Schools seem to me among the most anti-democratic, most authoritarian, most destructive, and most dangerous institutions of modern society. No other institution does more harm or more lasting harm to more people or destroys so much of their curiosity, independence, trust, dignity, and sense of identity and worth. Even quite kindly schools are inhibited and corrupted by the knowledge of children and teachers alike that they are *performing* for the judgement and approval of others—the children for the teachers; the teachers for the parents, supervisors, school board, or the state. No one is ever free from feeling that he is being judged all the time, or soon may be. Even after the best class experiences teachers must ask themselves, "Were we right to do that? Can we prove we were right? Will it get us in trouble?"

What corrupts the school, and makes it so much worse than most of the people in it, or than they would like it to be, is its power—just as their powerlessness corrupts the students. The school is corrupted by the endless anxious demand of the parents to know how their child is doing— meaning is he ahead of the other kids—and their demand that he be kept ahead. Schools do not protect children from the badness of the world outside. They are at least as bad as the world outside, and the harm they do to the children in their

247

power creates much of the badness of the world outside. The sickness of the modern world is in many ways a school-induced sickness. It is in school that most people learn to expect and accept that some expert can always place them in some sort of rank or hierarchy. It is in school that we meet, become used to, and learn to believe in the totally controlled society. We do not learn much science, but we learn to worship "scientists" and to believe that anything we might conceivably need or want can only come, and someday will come, from them. The school is the closest we have yet been able to come to Huxley's *Brave New World,* with its alphas and betas, deltas and epsilons—and now it even has its soma. Everyone, including children, should have the right to say "No!" to it.

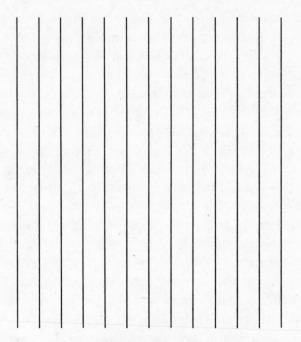

25. THE RIGHT TO USE DRUGS

Whatever rights the law grants to adults in the matter of drugs should be granted to the young. If a child is living as a dependent in his family's or guardian's home, the adults responsible for him should make the rules. If parents don't want a child to smoke *at home,* they have a right to say that or even to say don't smoke outside the house either. But it should be *their* business, not the business of the law and the police, to enforce it. Parents or other adults wanting to make rules for the young about drugs would have to use their own natural authority to enforce them.

On the whole I believe that people ought to be able to use the drugs they want. Those who sell drugs should be made by law to say what is in them and whatever is known about the short and long term effects of the drug. In short, the present requirement that sellers of tobacco say on each package that smoking may be injurious to your health does not seem nearly strong enough. It ought to say clearly that the chances are better than even that smoking over a number of years will greatly increase one's chances of getting heart attacks, emphysema, and cancer of the mouth, throat, or lungs. And perhaps, also, that nicotine is not only a cumulative poison but an addictive drug that produces withdrawal symptoms when people stop using it. This should also be required for such drugs as marijuana, coffee, alcohol, barbiturates, pep pills, tranquilizers, and all others. Any drug which is sold commercially, whether by prescription or otherwise, should have its properties, side effects, and possible dangers listed in some sort of directory available for the general public. Perhaps all stores selling such drugs might be required to have such a directory on the premises, and to show it to anyone asking to see it. Of course, about some drugs there will be a difference of opinion—as about Vitamin C or E, or Krebiozen, or others. In such cases there should be ways of making the pros and cons known to the potential buyer, who can then decide for himself. Many people feel that Vitamin C has helped them to have fewer colds. They should not be told that they can't use it because it has not been proven to help everyone.

This proposal, to allow all people to use what drugs they want, will of course be fought fiercely by people who will say that it only encourages "the drug culture," which they don't like and which they tend to associate with the young, minority groups, and other social outgroups and outcastes. They are right in one thing. We are indeed a drug culture. But this is nothing new and has little to do with the young. We were a drug culture long before the young started using drugs of their own and getting known for it. Most adults are regular and even heavy users of at least three psychoactive drugs—coffee, tobacco, and alcohol. All of these are powerful; all are to some extent addictive, not just psychologically but in a stricter sense; and all have dangerous side effects and are injurious to health, more so than at least some drugs that have been forbidden by law.

We might even add a fourth chemical to this list—sugar. If it is not addictive in the strict sense it is certainly psychologically addictive; most of our population, including children, are badly hooked on it. Thus in the August 23, 1973, issue of *New Scientist,* in an article entitled "Drugs and Public Morality," excerpted from the book *Medicine And Society* (Oxford University Press), Dr. Henry Miller says, in part:

> The very use of the term "drug" is emotive and begs the question. Alcohol and tobacco are by far the most important and most dangerous drugs used in the Western world, but they are not what the journalist has in mind when he discusses the problem of drug addicts. The employment of psychoactive substances is as old as recorded history, and there is no time or place where they have not been employed or where some have not been arbitrarily regarded as entirely acceptable, and the use of others as criminal.
>
> In the 19th century opium in one form or another was very widely used in Britain, especially by the poor and miserable,

and contemporary medical literature explains its superiority to alcohol in its effect on behavior. The same view was supported by Indian rulers who strongly resisted the introduction of spirits into their territories in favor of the retention of the opium habit. Much the same applies to cannabis; the Indian Hemp Commission of 1894 commented on the rarity of serious ill-effects, their limitation to the users of the drug, and the lack of any serious impact on society. [P. 442]

Indeed Dr. James Willis, in his recent book *Addicts* (Pitman Publishing) tells us that in part of India certain people who eat what most other people there consider too much of sweets and spicy snacks are seen as a kind of addict. This "addiction" is called "Chatorpan"; male addicts are called "chatora," female, "chatori." Conventional or respectable people take a very moralistic attitude toward these sweet-eaters. Thus Willis writes:

> . . . The people involved in chatorpan are generally considered by society to be rather worthless, immature people who are likely to be sexually promiscuous. The informants interviewed by the authors described neighbors who were excessive sweet-eaters as having entered into a process of moral and social deterioration. . . . the chronic sweet-eater is unable to afford his needs and will resort to cheating. stealing, and other means to obtain more money. Other informants described how chatoras engaged in criminal activity, and were frequently imprisoned. . . . it is the [chatora's] *excessive self-gratification* [italics mine] . . . that is supposed to lead to personal, moral, and social decline. [P. 40]

In addition, many adults take large amounts of other drugs. Millions are chronic users of aspirin, tranquilizers, pep pills, diet pills, sleeping pills. Bruce Jackson, in an article, "White Collar Pill Party," published in the *Atlantic* some years ago, reported that in one wealthy suburb of Chicago many rich and successful people regularly took prescription stimulants and sedatives in doses ten or twenty times greater than the maximum recommended dose. All of these drugs were, of course, prescribed for them by doctors. More recently *New York* magazine, and other publications, including *The New York Times,* have published articles about what are sometimes called Dr. Feelgoods—physicians who for a fee will shoot their patients with large doses of vitamins and some kind of amphetamine, what the young call "speed." Many prominent and powerful people have apparently frequently had such injections. Beyond all this there is a widespread feeling, encouraged by both advertising and the medical profession itself, that to be healthy you simply have a doctor tell you what is wrong with you and then give you a pill to fix it.

Those who have studied children who use drugs have found that many of them made their first experiments with drugs they found in their parents' medicine cabinets. Not long ago I read about one suburban town in which the latest kid's fad was a game called Goldfish. They come to a party or gathering, each with a bunch of pills from their parents' medicine cabinet. They put all these pills in a bowl and mix them up. Then each player or user puts in a hand and takes out five or six pills without looking, swallows them, and then waits to see what sort of effect he gets. The idea that all kinds of wonderful feelings can come from drugs is not something invented recently, or by the young.

Those who say that young people should not be allowed to smoke or drink often say that they are too young to know better. Do those who are older know better? Have *they* stopped smoking? They have not. According to a story in *The New York Times* of Nov. 5, 1973, both the total number of cigarettes smoked per year, and the number smoked per year per person over eighteen, have steadily risen since 1969, and the rate of increase itself seems to be rising. Forty-two percent of adult men and 30 percent of adult women smoke cigarettes; no figures are given for other kinds of smoking. If the problem is simply one of knowing what harm various drugs can do, we can easily tell people that when they are young. Even then there is not much evidence that warning children about the dangers of drugs will stop them from using them. Reports of so-called drug education programs in schools—which, by the way, say little about tobacco, alcohol, and coffee—and about the effect of these programs on young people show, first, that the young don't believe most of what the adults tell them and, secondly, that what they do believe makes them curious about these drugs and eager to use them, perhaps on the theory that if the teachers and parents are all against them they can't be all bad. One writer has said that of course young people know these drugs are dangerous, *that's why they use them.* Many states, New York for one, require that schools teach all pupils the dangers of alcohol. Do people in such states drink less then those in states without such programs? And what of the legislators themselves who vote for such programs? We can be sure that most of them are drinkers.

In any case, since the people who do supposedly know about the harmful effects of alcohol, tobacco, coffee, sugar, sleeping pills, and pep pills go on using them, and more every year, what reason is there to say that young people should be forbidden to use them until they are "old enough to know better"? Some might say that the young will make even worse choices about using these drugs than adults. But in their terms there can be no worse choice than the one adults have made, which is to use them. Others might say that certain drugs will do more harm to growing children even than to adults—stunt their growth, injure their hearts. If this is true, makers and suppliers of drugs should have to make it known to everyone, including the young.

In any case, there is no reason to believe that telling children that they can't smoke until they are older will reduce their desire to do it, either at the time or when they are older. No one likes his first smoke—or his second, third, or tenth. The taste is terrible, the sensations (if you inhale and succeed in not coughing or choking) are strong and unpleasant and the aftertaste is bad. It takes persistence to get this habit. Why do young people persist? Because it is a sign of being grown-up, in a world where there are few other signs. Also, they see all those adults doing it, so in spite of what their senses tell them they think there must be something in it and that if they only stick at it long enough they will find out. Before too long, like their elders, they are hooked. But younger children are more ready to respect their senses. When something tastes bad to them, they do not go on tasting it but refuse it. If we really wanted young people not to smoke, we could probably do no better than to treat smoking the way we do reading—make every child smoke a cigarette or two each day in school and humiliate and punish those who did not, could not, or *refused* to finish their assigned cigarettes.

Right now many children smoke (both tobacco and

marijuana) and drink, and not just in the home, long before the law permits. Most children have smoked tobacco (probably marijuana) before they are twelve years old, and many smoke frequently; most have drunk some alcohol by that time; and many, or perhaps, most by the age of fourteen or fifteen have had the experience of being somewhat drunk. Perhaps if they were allowed they might smoke and drink even more. This still does not seem a good or sufficient reason for trying to forbid it. My own belief is that young people smoke and drink too much as a way of trying to *look* grown-up in a society in which there is no real and serious way to *be* grown-up. Or they are driven to do this by social pressure from their peer groups, in order to show their courage in a society in which there is no serious and authentic way to do so. Or they do it simply to annoy and frighten the adults on the principle "If you can't join them, lick them."

If young people give in so easily to social pressure from their peer group, perhaps it is because it is the only group they can join. They have hardly any chance, are hardly even allowed, to associate with anyone else. When they do meet adults, it is as children, subordinates and inferiors, without knowledge, worth, dignity, or rights. They have almost no serious contact with people who might exert a counterpressure, if only in the form of a better example. They rarely meet someone older they would not want to disappoint or sadden by stupid or destructive behavior. Those are rare and fortunate young people who know even one adult whom they like, trust, and respect enough to want to preserve his good opinion of them.

When I was young I drank, and almost always and

deliberately too much, only in certain kinds of competitive social situations—parties, dances, and so forth—where I felt so ill at ease that I drank to get the feeling of assurance that I (wrongly) thought everyone else had. But the social functions and competitiveness themselves were the cause of the trouble. In a society more respectful of children there would be many more occasions in which people of different ages mixed, where the whole question of status was not so important, and where older and more experienced and kindly people could make it easier for young people to enter into a larger society. When I was young I always felt more at ease and had more fun at gatherings where most of the people were older; I didn't have to worry about being popular.

Children often have more sensible attitudes toward alcohol in families that do not make it something mysterious and forbidden. In such families even very young children are allowed to have a taste of whatever the adults are drinking. Until the age of about five, they usually like most of this; after that, they dislike it very much and are not interested in it until many years later. They are allowed to have a little wine or champagne on special occasions. At the age of twelve or so they may be invited to have a glass of beer with their parents and guests when they are drinking. Such children are less apt to think of drinking as some magical proof of being grown-up and may have less craving to do it. Also, they know something of the effect that it has on them and may use it a bit more wisely.

In short, I don't think we should "protect" children against whatever drugs their elders use, and in a society in which most of their elders do use drugs and many use them excessively and unwisely, I don't see how we can. Some years

257

ago there was a great scandal in France; investigators found that in some parts of the country many children had become alcoholics before they were ten. The explanation was simple enough. In those parts of the country the adults drank nothing but wine, hard cider, and brandy. Children are active, they get thirsty, they need to drink a lot of something; and if all they can find to drink is alcohol, many of them will become alcoholics. The best and only protection against this danger is a plentiful supply of other good things to drink. Beyond that we might offer children (1) adequate information about what they are using; (2) the example of adults who are themselves not drug-addicted; (3) a society in which there are better ways of being adult than using drugs; (4) a society in which life is not so dull, pointless, hopeless, or horrifying that people will take drugs to escape the pain of it.

Our schools themselves have often helped spread the use of drugs among the young. This is partly because as a meeting place for the young they are a center of supply. In that sense, we might say that the school has replaced the old corner drug store—it now *is* the drug store. Also, it is a place where young people can talk to others about their own use of drugs, compare sensations and effects. In addition, the mean-spirited, status-seeking competitiveness of the schoolroom spills over into the area of drug use so that young people who are urged to compete with each other in their studies and to win at each others' expense bring this competitiveness into their use of drugs, taking this drug or that to show that they are bolder or more experimental than the others. The school is itself often so boring, anxious, ugly, and punitive that many young people say they take drugs, right in the school building, just to help them get through the school day. In this respect, as in many others, the school is very like the factory, where there is also widespread and increasing drug use.

As Dr. Thomas Szasz has often pointed out, even heroin was for some time a legal drug in this country. Many otherwise respectable people used it, and many of them lived otherwise normal and productive lives. It is not, or not necessarily, true that using heroin makes it impossible for people to function in normal situations. Even today some heroin users hold jobs, or they do as long as they can keep their use a secret—if it gets out, they get fired, which then really does make them into a social problem. Nor is it true that heroin, of and by itself, is necessarily the life-destroying drug that our officials and press make it out to be. One researcher, a doctor, wrote not long ago that in terms of its immediate and long-run effects heroin, if pure, is one of the least harmful drugs that man has ever put into his system. It is the heroin way of life, the terrible difficulty and expense of getting the drug, more than the drug itself that destroys life—that, and the fact that the drug itself is so often cut or diluted with other and far more dangerous drugs. Thus, many addicts who die from what is called an overdose of heroin in fact die from quinine or other kinds of poisoning. To kill oneself with pure heroin would require a dose much larger than most addicts could ever afford. By itself heroin was probably a good deal less destructive to health than tobacco or alcohol. But it gave users quick and cheap pleasure, which in a Puritan country was itself bad, and it made them unambitious and passive, which seemed even worse. What really enraged most people about heroin (and marijuana) was and is the belief that when people take it they don't want to work. So the public was sold the idea that heroin use was a terrible danger, and laws were passed outlawing it. Thus the heroin controlling industry was born, now a big business, and the heroin-supplying industry, now an even bigger business. (The two businesses at many levels interconnect.) But there is little reason to believe that the use of the drug itself was at first an important health problem. When heroin was legal the highest estimate was that we had in the country 200,000 habitual users—what we now call addicts. Compare this with our present *nine million* alcoholics or even the 50,000 people killed each year, and the many times that number seriously injured, in auto accidents.

Now and then some anti-heroin expert or bureaucrat says that other countries have tried the experiment of making heroin legal, and that it hasn't "worked." When we ask, "What do you mean, it hasn't worked, in what way hasn't it worked?" they say it hasn't worked because people are still using heroin, perhaps even more than they used to. This is what is called in logic "begging the question." When people can use heroin, some of them do, because they like it. This is exactly the reason for which most people use coffee, or tobacco, or alcohol. If some people can put some drugs—powerful, psychoactive, addictive—into their systems just because they like them, why can't other people do the same with other drugs for the same reason? *

Recent reports tend to show that as heroin gets more expensive and scarce, and of poorer quality, more and more people are switching to other, more easily available, drugs,

* An excellent, and perhaps the most recent and balanced comparison between the British and American ways of dealing with heroin, appeared in a two-part article, *The British and Heroin,* by Horace Freeland Judson, in the "Reporter At Large" section of *The New Yorker,* for September 24 and October 1, 1973.

notably barbiturates, sedatives, and tranquilizers. This is a far more serious health hazard than heroin ever was. The barbiturates are not cumulative poisons; the body can get rid of them in its normal processes. If someone takes an overdose, one has only to keep them alive and awake for eight hours or so to bring them out of danger. This is not true of many of the newer sedatives, tranquilizers, and hypnotic drugs, which stay in the body so that those who take an overdose, if they survive at all, may need intensive and expensive care for as much as two weeks.

It is frequently estimated that about two-thirds of the legal production of stimulants and depressants now find their way into the black market. This makes the "control" of these drugs almost impossible. Also, not only is there a very large supply of these "legal" drugs available, but there are almost infinite possibilities for combining these. One popular combination, barbiturates—i.e., sleeping pills—and alcohol, is very dangerous, far more so than either could be alone.

It is also true that many of these drugs are not very hard to make—people who know some chemistry could make them with equipment that could easily fit into a room in a house. This was true of LSD, for example. The demand for LSD has gone down, partly because so much of it became so contaminated that the drug got a bad name among users, partly because other drugs have become more fashionable. But if the fashions change again there will be plenty of small-scale suppliers of this drug. The same is certainly true of many others. And no one in drug rehabilitation work seems to think that there is any way to dry up the huge supply of drugs that come from the big drug companies. In short, the attempt to control drugs by cutting off the supply, and by making their use illegal, seems as sure to fail as Prohibition and has so far led to the same results—the growth of a huge and criminal supplying industry, an increase in the power of the police to meddle in the private lives of citizens, and the growing violence and corruption of police and law-enforcement officials themselves.

Recently a number of publications, including *The New York Times,* have printed some horrifying articles about the illegal, violent, and often murderous acts of narcotics agents. In case after case these agents, without warrants or any kind of court order, often without evidence or probable cause, going only on hunch or rumor, usually without uniforms or identification, have smashed their way into houses in the middle of the night, threatened, abused, and terrorized the owners, and in some cases have shot and killed those who quite naturally resisted or ran away. Often they prove to have gone to the wrong house altogether. Or, if they have gone to the house they were looking for, there has been absolutely nothing there to justify the raid. And when in the course of these violent and illegal raids agents do kill an innocent person, as in a recent and shocking case in Humboldt County, California, they go unpunished—indeed, one court in San Francisco made the grotesque finding that the murdered young man had not had his civil rights violated. To which we can only ask, if policemen in disguise, without evidence or warrant, can make an armed and unprovoked attack on our homes and kill us without "violating our civil rights," exactly what civil rights do we have left? Our anti-drug laws, and the hysteria behind them, invite this sort of legalized murder, and we can expect to have more of it.

A story entitled "Drug Raid Victims Strive to Construct

a New Life" by Andrew Malchilm in *The New York Times* of Sunday, August 19, 1973, told of the aftermath of one of these illegal and violent drug raids. The story says, in part:

> Herbert and Evelyn Gigliotto, the Collinsville, Ill. couple who fled their home after an illegal government drug raid *and subsequent harassment* [italics mine] are struggling to begin a new life in an undisclosed western community.

> . . . 15 agents of the Federal Office for Drug Abuse Law Enforcement . . . operating without a search warrant and without their superior's permission . . . broke into the apartment late one night, screamed obscenities, held the couple at gunpoint in their beds and ransacked the two-bedroom dwelling before discovering that they had the wrong address. No drugs were found.

> The Gigliottos sued for $1 million. . . . The Federal Drug Enforcement Administration has begun action to dismiss six of the narcotics agents. . . .

> After the Gigliottos had told about the raid, they received anonymous late night telephone calls. Both their cars were damaged while parked. The car of Mr. Gigliotto's brother was slashed. And someone recently tried to break into the home of Mr. Gigliotto's mother in a nearby Illinois town.

> "So in early July we had it and decided to move," Mr. Gigliotto said as he relaxed in the living room of his newly rented house. The Gigliottos asked that the address of their new home not be published.

> "Maybe we accomplished something by bringing these raids to light, but they've just ruined our lives," said the 31-year-old boilermaker who had been unable to find any employment since he quit his Illinois job. . . .

This is an extraordinary story, to say the least. It has not been proven, but there is certainly every reason to believe that the drug agents themselves, or others known to them and allied with them, were responsible for the harassment that drove the Gigliottos from their jobs and home. Is this where we have come, that agents of the government, having once attacked us criminally, will attack us again for reporting them? That a citizen who has reported the illegal acts of government agents must then go into hiding for his safety, as if *he* were the criminal? Perhaps this story has not ended, but that is where it stands now.

In any case, laws controlling drug use by adults will probably do little good and much harm, and laws denying to children the right to do what adults can do will have the same effect. Even if it were true that the mere use of drugs by citizens is some sort of "problem," a bad thing that ought not to happen, the only answer to this "problem" is to create a world and society in which the undrugged life is so interesting, beautiful, and worthwhile, that people will be glad to live without drugs. If most people knew what it felt like to be in really good physical condition and, beyond that, lived in a place they liked and did work that they really loved doing, they would probably find, most of the time, that drugs made them feel not better but worse. But most people have not known since they were about six years old, if then, what it was like to be in a state of full health, energy, and contact with the world, what Andrew Weil in *The Natural Mind* calls "a natural high." The problem is to create a society and encourage ways of living in which people will keep through most of their lives the health, energy, and alertness that they felt when they were six.

Even then, in any society we might construct, however

good, many people, at least for certain occasions, might want to use drugs. In all his cultures and history, man seems to have been as much a drug-using as a tool-using animal. Perhaps he always will be so.

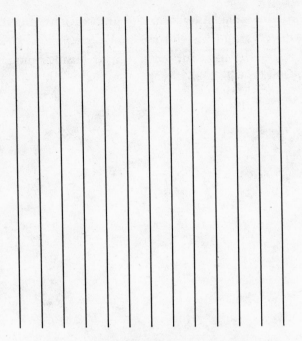

26. THE RIGHT TO DRIVE

Most states, perhaps under some pressure from adults who do not want any longer to have to be their children's chauffeurs, and perhaps also under some pressure from the auto industry and its various lobbies, allow young people the right to drive before they allow them any other of the rights of adults. In many and perhaps most states, young people may legally drive a car some years before they may legally buy a pack of cigarettes from a vending machine—which is, to say the least, absurd. My own belief is that tests for a driver's license should be made harder, that people should have to take them more often, and that people should much more easily than now, and for a wider range of driving offenses, lose their licenses. But anyone, of whatever age, who can show that he has the knowledge and skill to drive a car safely and well ought to be allowed to drive it.

Many people quote figures that show that people under twenty-five get into more accidents than older drivers. They argue that since driving is a matter of judgement and that since this judgement comes only with age, we would do better to raise, not lower, the legal driving age. To this I would say first that even if the figures show what people claim, it is grossly unjust to discriminate in law against anyone merely because he is a member of a statistical group. Statistics do not prove, and could never prove, that just because a person is under twenty-five he is a bad driver, or worse than older drivers. Because of his better eyesight and reflexes, he might very well be better. Judgements like these, if they must be made, must be made not on groups but on individuals.

There are many steps we could take to cut the dreadful toll of death and injury on our highways that would be far more effective than discriminating against the young. Indeed, they would save many of the children who as passengers are now injured and killed in auto accidents. These would include: (1) stiffer driving tests; (2) much stiffer and non-escapable penalties for driving under the influence of alcohol; (3) better designed and built cars, that is, cars with much better braking and handling; (4) more crash-resistant cars, such as Rover, Volvo, and Mercedes-Benz have had on the market for years; (5) less powerful cars and strict limitations on power; (6) strict requirements for the provision and use of lap and shoulder belts and stricter penalties for not using them; (7) much stricter accountability for car makers and dealers; thus, there ought to be made public, which has not been done, known facts about the extent to which accidents are caused by defects in the cars themselves and *which* cars are most involved in accidents; (8) lower speed limits where accidents are known to occur and other speed limiting devices, such as roughness, bumps, built into road surfaces so that people who will not slow down to save their lives may slow down to save their cars; (9) financial rewards of one kind or another for people who drive without getting into accidents; (10) very strict re-testing for people involved in accidents or guilty of safety violations; (11) much more rigorous and honest safety inspection. And more effective than any of these would be to do what we should do for many other reasons, and may soon be compelled to do because of a lack of fuel—cut down on the total amount of cars and driving, make it harder to get to places in cars and easier to get there in other, cheaper, safer ways.

One more thing ought to be said about young people and their driving and drinking. It is not just because they are young and inexperienced, or lack judgement, that young people drink and/or drive unwisely. They do this more out of bravado than ignorance. They know that what they are doing is dangerous and they do it for that reason. For many young people, probably men more so than women, driving and drinking, or both, are ways of *seeming* to act grown-up, of proving one's toughness and courage. But this is all pretend, as it has to be in a society that allows and gives the young no real way to be grown-up and no worthy tests of their ability and courage. If we took a sensible rather than romantic view of cars, designed them to be reliable and safe rather than manhood-sex-success-glamor symbols, kept them under proper control, if most adults drove moderately and safely, and if the young were not shut out of adult society but welcomed into it as soon and as far as they were ready to go —in such a situation most young people would probably drive as well as their elders and because of better eyesight, reflexes, and coordination, many of them might drive much better.

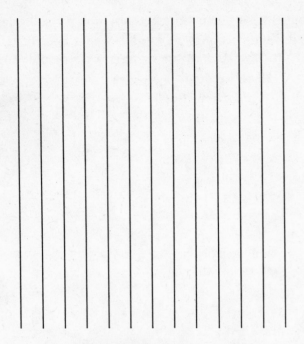

27. THE LAW, THE YOUNG, AND SEX

All people, including young people, should have the right to control their own private sex lives and acts. It is not the proper business of the state or government to pry into such matters. I agree with those who now say that whatever consenting adults want to do privately in the matter of sex they should be allowed to do, and that it is theirs and nobody else's business. If and when the law allows people at earlier ages than now to choose to become independent and responsible citizens, I would want these citizens to have the same rights in the matter of sex as any other citizens, regardless of age. Later I will discuss the perhaps harder question of the rights of young people who are not citizens, but living as dependents with some sort of guardians.

One reason we do not now grant these rights to adults, far less to young people, is that many people feel that anything to do with sex is somehow dirty, bad, and wrong. We are both a prurient and puritan society, a very dangerous mixture. In many places in the U.S. an effective political majority believes that sex is by right, and ought to be by law, illegal except to beget children within wedlock or perhaps to serve as the glue that holds together the institution of marriage and that all other sexual acts should be punishable by law. Perhaps like many other attitudes these will only change as the people who hold them die and are replaced by others with different attitudes. It seems likely that even if a changing society grants to the young many other of the rights I propose, this right will be one of the very last they grant.

Another reason why we shrink from giving children control of their sex lives is that many of us, including many whose views on adult sex are quite liberal, still believe and need to believe that children are "innocent" and "pure," that is, asexual, untainted by sexual thoughts, feelings or urges. There is increasing evidence that this is not true even of very young children, and it is certainly not true of children much past the age of ten or eleven. Many studies seem to show that young people are reaching puberty at even earlier ages. But we cling to this view of children for many reasons, not the least of which is that pretending they have no sexual feeling makes it easier for us to ignore or deny the sexual part of their attraction for us. We feel free to use them as love objects partly because we can tell ourselves that, since it is impossible, it would never occur to us to use them, or them to use us, as sex objects.

Some say that since women must bear the consequences of sex—pregnancy and childbirth—the law must protect them against sex, above all if they are young, lest they become pregnant against their will. This makes some sense in a society that, like most today, has not yet allowed women to decide whether they will have children or not, or how many, but instead treats them in this respect as baby-producing machines controlled by men and the state. Right now many young women in increasing numbers, in spite of (or perhaps because of) the law, and at earlier and earlier ages, become pregnant without wanting to, and must bear children they do not want and don't know what to do with. This causes them, and certainly the children, many serious social and emotional problems, from which any humane person would want to spare them. Beyond this there is increasing evidence that early pregnancies, like very late ones, are much more likely to produce defective children.

We could easily avert these problems, dangers, and tragedies if we told children when they were young, or simply let them find out, about sex, procreation, birth, and contraception. If by the age of ten all young people knew how pregnancies occur and how they can be prevented, if birth control materials and advice were widely and cheaply available to any and all who asked for them, if beyond that we developed, as we probably could, a safer and easily available retroactive or after-the-event birth control pill, or an effective male contraceptive, there would be almost no unwanted pregnancies. If we also developed and made available safe, easy, and cheap ways to end such unwanted pregnancies as did occur, there would be very few unwanted children. Then at least this reason for thinking that we have to protect in-experienced young girls from the perils of sex would no longer have weight.

Some people have voiced to me the fear that if it were legal for an adult to have sex with a consenting child, many young people would be exploited by unscrupulous older ones. The image here is of the innocent young girl and the dirty old man; few worry about the young boy having sex with an older woman. Here, too, we are caught with the re-mains of old myths—in this case, that only men were sexual, that women were pure and above it—from which it follows that any young girl having sex with an older man must neces-sarily be his victim.

A mother of three daughters told me once that because she, speaking for society, was able to tell one of her daughters that she could not sleep with a young man who wanted to sleep with her and was using various kinds of blackmail in order to get her to do it, the daughter was protected. She did not have to say no for herself. She could even say things like, "I'd like to but my mother would kill me." But this is all in the context of a society in which men exploit women as sex objects. In a society such as I propose, the dangers (to the daughter) of sex would be less. At the same time the pres-sure on the young man to make a conquest would also be much less. If sex were not seen as dangerous, romantic, and ecstatic, and at the same time dirty and disgusting, there would be less need to protect people from it, and they would be more able to protect themselves. Women who did not feel that their worth depended on their being sexually attractive to men would not be swayed by the kind of blackmail boys use on girls today—indeed, they would be turned away by it. A young man who tried it would soon be out of luck.

But if young people living as independent and responsible citizens have the same rights as any other citizens in matters of sex, should those still living as dependents have the right to control their own sex lives? Should their guardians have any say in the matter? If they disagree, should the law step in, and if so, how?

I find myself in a number of tensions or internal conflicts here. I don't want the state to have any *more* power over the private lives of people, including young people, than it now has. By the same token, I don't want anyone, young or old, to have *less* control of his sex life than he has now. In short, I don't want the law to say that young people should not have the right to do what in fact a great many of them do right now. But it is not easy to know what power the state now has and, therefore, what rights the young now have.

Many of our laws on sexual conduct are a dead letter; they are not enforced and few now intend or expect them to be. They stay on the books because it is politically safer for legislators to ignore them than to try to get them repealed, which would make some people accuse them of advocating sexual license. Many have written that if all the laws about sex now on the books were rigorously and impartially enforced, most of the population would be in jail. Fortunately the state does not try to prevent what the law forbids, and much of what it tries to prevent it is not able to prevent; more and more young people, and earlier and earlier, do have sexual relations with each other in spite of difficulties, danger, and the law itself. This is fine with me. When the state is trying to do what it ought not to do, the less effectively it does it, the better. On the other hand, I don't like dead-letter laws, laws which the state does not mean to enforce but does not dare to repeal. They invite selective enforcement. There is too great a danger that they will some-day be used to harass and even jail whoever the state does not happen to like. The law should be explicit and should mean what it says; but any attempt to do this now in the area of sex could only result in giving the state more power rather than less, in matters where it should have none.

Another tension is this. On the one hand it seems to me that to have sexual relations with another person should be a responsible rather than casual act, since it is almost sure to have emotional consequences even if physical ones can be controlled or prevented. From this it would follow that sexual freedom should be the right only of those who have chosen to be responsible in other respects, to be independent citizens. But this would mean that it was forbidden to all young people living as dependents. Whose job would it be to prevent it, and how would they do it? This could only lead to continued prying, poking, snooping, moralizing, and threatening by adults, which would be no more effective than it is now but would, as it does now, poison the relationships between the old and young. The remedy seems worse than the ill. Worse yet, it would continue the evil we have today, that many young girls are put in prison for years for having or seeming to have sexual relations with young men. This we should at all cost prevent. For the state to deprive someone of liberty by putting him in prison is a most serious act, close to a crime in itself. It can only be justified by the most weighty cause, that the prisoner did real harm to others. But to make the act of sex, the mutual giving and receiving of pleasure, the excuse for putting someone in prison seems both mistaken and morally wrong.

Still another tension. On the one hand, it seems only right and fair that as long as a young person has chosen to remain a child, dependent on his parents or other guardians, his sex life, at least in their house, should be their business. If they approve of, or at least don't mind, his having sexual relations with others, there is no problem. But if they dislike it or disapprove of it, there is no reason why they should have to allow it to go on under their noses. Secondary guardians could of course say, "What you do with your sex life is your business, but what happens in this house is our business, and we don't want it here, and if you won't go along with that, you'll have to leave." They might even say, "While you are our ward, we don't want you to do it anywhere, we don't approve of it, and it gives us a bad name with other people." If the parents or guardians, in the eyes of everyone else and themselves, are responsible for what their children do, then in important matters they should have some right to tell the children what to do or not to do. Except of course, with respect to those rights of the child, such as the right to vote or work, that are specifically guaranteed by the state. If the children don't want to live by their parents' rules, and can't persuade them to change them, they have always the choice of seeking out other guardians or living an independent life.

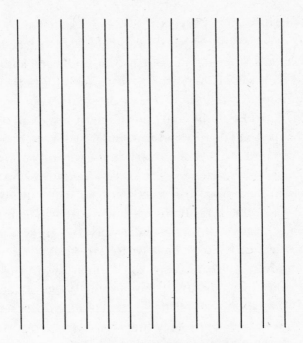

28. STEPS TO TAKE

Paul Goodman, in his many talks with young people, used to say that one good way to work for a truly different and better world was to act in their daily lives, as far as they could, as if that world existed. What would you do, he would ask them, if the world had become more or less the kind of place you want it to be; how would you live, how would you treat other people? Live that way now, treat them that way now. If something prevents you, try to find a way to deal with that. We can begin to treat children, even the youngest and smallest, wherever we may find them, as we would want everyone to treat them in the society we are trying to make.

We can begin by trying to be courteous to them. This will be very difficult for those who have been taught by experience only to be servile to the strong and rude and bossy toward the weak or those who have learned to think of children as love objects and to treat them as they would a favorite dog or cat. For to be courteous we must first of all respect the other person's dignity and sense of self. We must treat him with a certain formality and reserve until we find out how he would like to be treated. We must respect not just his physical but his emotional life space until he shows us how far into that space he is ready to welcome us. And though being courteous means much more than merely being polite, it means at least that. So we must try to learn to say "Please" or "Excuse Me" or "Thank You" to children, and in the same tone of voice we would use to anyone else. We must not treat a child like a servant and demand from him favors or services that we would not think of asking of someone our own age. Indeed, because he is new in this world, and gets his sense of it from how we behave toward him, we would do well to show him extra courtesy like the wise parents who said to me once that most of the time they tried to behave toward their then four-year-old son as if he were a very distinguished visitor from a strange and alien civilization, knowing little but eager to learn about how we do things here.

Another small way to be courteous is by respecting and protecting the child's right to privacy. Until the law gives to him as it does to us (at least on paper) the right to be free from arbitrary search and seizure, we should act as if he had that right. This means, among other things, not going into a child's room without asking, and receiving, permission. Many children's rooms have signs saying, "Keep Out!," "Danger," "Absolutely Private," and the like. This fierceness may amuse us but it may well be a child's desperate clutch at a privacy and dignity he has never had and does not expect to get. Many children who put up such signs know that they won't be respected, that "their" room is as open to other people as any room in their house.

And privacy means privacy of thought as well as space. Too many people think they have a right and duty to know almost everything their child is doing or even thinking. They ask, "What did you do in school today?" to which the child very often replies, "Nothing." He only means, "Nothing that I want to talk about." Or perhaps, "Nothing that I want (or dare) talk to you about—at least right now." People who really like hearing what their children have been doing don't usually have to ask them.

I have already suggested some ways in which we might encourage and help children to be more informed, competent, and independent. Let me suggest a few more. People often claim that if children could own and spend their own money as they pleased, they would spend it foolishly, would be cheated, would buy what they could not pay for. Only recently one man asked me, "Why wouldn't a child take a credit card to the candy store and there buy ten-dollars worth of jelly beans?" Questions like this, which show the fear and contempt many people feel for children, are quite common. I said that I had never known a child to buy ten-dollars worth of jelly beans all at once and doubted that any child ever had. Even if one did, he might learn many things from the experience. He might learn that ten-dollars worth of jelly beans is more that he would want or could stand to eat. He might try to sell the surplus to friends at school, might even make a little profit. He might only learn that buying nothing but jelly beans is a stupid way to spend ten dollars. But it is hard to see how he could be much hurt by the experience.

Still, a child growing up in a culture where money is important has much to learn about money, what people have to do to get it, how much they get for what they can do, what they can buy with it, and how they take care of it. Most families do not make available to children experiences from which they might learn such things. Most children know little or nothing about the work their fathers and/or mothers do, or how much they are paid for it, or how this money is spent. I doubt that most children know such things today. But many would like to and it would be better if they did.

Beyond letting the child see how the family finances work, we could as soon as possible, give him the choice of controlling and spending some or all of the money we now spend on him. For years many middle-class parents have given their children, even when quite young, an allowance. But this is usually a small sum, to be spent on trivia—though some thrifty children will save it for a long time to buy something more important. Some older children are given a larger allowance, from which to buy their clothes, entertainment, and the like. Even then the parents still buy for these children much of what they need and rarely ask them to account for what they spend themselves. We could go further than this. Parents could keep track for a year or two, perhaps with the help of the child, of all the money they spend on his needs. Then they could offer to put this much money into a special account under his control and let him buy these needs for himself. Many children might not care to do this, but those who did would learn important things about making priorities and choices—things better learned sooner than later. The point is always to offer the child the chance to take greater responsibilty and to make more serious choices.

Earlier I said that children need, and ought to be encouraged and helped to have, more adult friends or friends of different ages than themselves. Today, on the whole, we discourage this; there are very few people we will *allow* our children to know. The only friends we want a child to have are other children his own age or perhaps the older or younger children of our own friends. The only adults we want him to know are our friends or the parents of his friends. These will in turn see him only as the child of their friends or the friend of their children, rarely as a person in his own right. Thus suppose Mr. and Mrs. Smith, who have an eight-year-old son, Tom, call up Mr. and Mrs. Jones, whom they don't know, to ask if they can take their son, Sam, to a picnic, movie, sports event, or whatever. The Joneses will probably think this is all right, though they will assume that Tom Smith is going along too. But suppose Mr. and Mrs. Smith have no children of Sam Jones' age or, worse yet, no children at all. The Joneses would then think this invitation very strange and would probably not let Sam go. If it is a single Mr. or Miss Smith doing the inviting or if the Joneses' child were a girl, they would be even more alarmed.

Children are told all the time not to talk to, or have anything to do with, "strangers," by which we mean everyone except the friends of their parents or the parents of their friends. Everyone else is taboo. Thus we allow children only a very limited range of relationships with adults. The reason for such fears is, of course, that every so often some older person kidnaps and rapes, abuses, or kills a young child. This is horrifying, but we would probably find that the number of children abused or killed by such strangers is only a small fraction of the number killed or maimed and crippled in auto accidents. And in trying to protect them against "strangers," by denying them the right to make their own older friends and to know a variety of people of different ages, we all may be doing children a very great harm.

To change these and other public attitudes will be very hard, harder even than changing attitudes about schools and schooling. People have been talking and arguing about schools for decades. But the ideas and attitudes about children that I hope to see change are ones that few people have talked or even thought much about. At this stage perhaps the most important thing we can do is make these ideas better known. At the same time we should try to make it possible for any children under our control, if they want to, to go more places, know more people, make more choices, do more things—in short, to free them more and more from their dependence on us. In our private lives, even in a society with generally opposed laws and attitudes, there is much here that we can do.

What we can do in the public or political area is in part suggested by a story entitled "Less School—More Work" in the August 27, 1973, issue of *Time* magazine, which says in part:

> "With every decade, the length of schooling has increased, until a thoughtful person must ask whether society can conceive of no other way for youth to come into adulthood." So writes Sociologist James Coleman, chairman of the Panel on Youth of the President's Science Advisory Committee. . . . In a new report [Coleman] and his team of nine social scientists and educators recommend more work and less school for young Americans aged 14 to 24.

. . . schools are not designed to provide such adult necessities as the ability to manage one's own affairs or to engage in "intense concentrated involvement in an activity." Nor are they the place for learning how to take responsibility for and work with others.

Schools not only fail to develop these capabilities, says the Coleman panel, but by monopolizing young people's time, they also prevent them from acquiring skills elsewhere. . . .

. . . the best remedy is to limit schooling, and provide opportunities for the young to alternate study with work. Participation in serious and responsible work with people of different backgrounds and ages would promote adult capabilities and counteract the isolation and passivity of school.

The panel's most provocative proposal is to get the young out of schools earlier and into other organizations. Hospitals, symphony orchestras, department stores and factories all are urged to experiment with such a plan, taking on youngsters from age 16, using them for whatever labor they can perform, while teaching them further skills and overseeing their formal schooling. . . . It might also move toward an even older pattern—apprenticeship.

Coleman himself goes beyond the panel's proposal to urge the development of working communities that encompass all ages. An organization of 1,000 persons five to 13 and 100 oldsters over 65. . . .

This is of course exactly what Paul Goodman wrote and talked about for years. It is encouraging that a committee this close to the center of political power should support these ideas. This does not necessarily mean that anyone in government is going to do anything about them. But it does give us something to refer to when we talk to people with political power, a sign that we are not crackpots. Making these ideas look respectable does not guarantee that they will be acted on, but they will surely not be acted on if they do not look respectable.

The next part of the *Time* article, entitled "If You Can Find It," suggests one of the kinds of steps we might take, at the federal level, or in our cities and states.

> For the past three years the government of Canada has funded an innovative program called Opportunities for Youth, which pays students to dream up and work at jobs they want to do—such as bike patrols for cyclists in distress or day camps for children of low-income families.

Such job or work programs should not be controlled by the schools or else being able to work, and to define your own work, may become a reward for doing well in school. This would insure that opportunities for work, like most present "enrichment programs" in schools, go least to those who need them most.

There are many organizations now that need and would welcome the help that young people could give—small newspapers and magazines, film or theatre groups, small independent schools, organizations working for unpopular causes. There are many lists or directories of such organizations and places to work. One of the first was (and is) Vocations For Social Change, of Canyon, California. Since then there have been many others, so many that at least one publication, *Somewhere Else*, (Box 350, Evanston, Illinois 60204) has set out to list all these sources of information. In most large cities, or in college or university towns, some bookstores will carry such lists. Many more young people than now would be glad to spend some time working with these organizations, or doing many other kinds of useful work, even without pay, if they could get school credit for doing it, or even without school credit, if they could legally get out of school to do it. The school attendance laws of our states should be changed to make this possible.

We can also work, again largely in the state legislatures, to correct some of the grossest abuses of the civil liberties of young people. One of the worst of these is the practice of what is called "corporal punishment" in schools, but what might better be called legalized assault by adults against children—most often the children of the poor and of minority groups. This practice is legal in most states and, at least until very recently, was widely practiced in at least one state, Massachusetts, in which it is not legal. Enough has been said about this brutal and disgusting practice, most notably in Jonathan Kozol's book *Death at an Early Age,* so that there is no need to add to it here. There has now been formed the National Committee to Abolish Corporal Punishment in Schools, which publishes a newsletter (Editor, Donna Hazouri; Emory University, Atlanta, Georgia 30322). Another group is the Committee to End Violence Against the Next Generation (977 Keeler Avenue, Berkeley, California 94708).

In a broader sense we must see to it that the law no longer punishes young people more severely than it does adults or that young people who are in the hands of the state, often without having committed any crimes or done anything at all, are not brutalized but are humanely treated. An organization devoted to these ends is the Institute for Juvenile Justice, P.O. Box 2101, Albuquerque, New Mexico, or 540 East 13th Street, New York, New York 10009.

It may be useful to try to have introduced in many legislatures bills that would make available to the young some or all of the rights I have proposed, even if there is at first little chance of these bills passing. It would get the bills talked about, it might draw some useful publicity, it would give an opportunity to testify in support of the bills before legislative committees, and it might turn up sympathetic legislators with whom we could then work over the years for further legislation.

Beyond this, certain bills may be politically feasible in the near future. Thus, in a number of states we might be able to lower the age of legal majority to eighteen. We might get laws passed giving the rights to work, and to live as independent citizens, at an age younger than eighteen, to those young people without families who are now living as wards or prisoners of the state. We might pass a law, as was done in Massachusetts, requiring schools to make available to parents of children, or the children themselves if over eighteen, all records kept on them by the school; and we might further extend this right to see school records for children much younger than eighteen. We might pass laws enlarging the right of young people to bring suit against adults. This might be particularly effective against the more severe forms of child abuse; even the most hot-headed parent might hesitate to throw his child down the stairs or out the window if he knew that the child, if not killed, might sue him for heavy damages. There is much to be done.

Let me close by saying what I hope I have already made clear. I know very well that modern childhood is hard on adults as well as children, that it is as hard to raise a child as to be a child, and is getting harder all the time. I hope that what I propose may soon make it easier for both of them.

ABOUT THE AUTHOR

John Holt has taught in Colorado, Massachusetts, and California. He has assisted elementary school children and Harvard graduate students. Mr. Holt's books, *How Children Learn, How Children Fail, The Underachieving School, What Do I Do Monday?*, and *Freedom And Beyond*, and his articles in *The New York Times Magazine, Harper's, The New York Review of Books, The Grade Teacher*, and many other publications, have become standard works in the field of education.